Read Real
NIHONGO

Japanese texts
for intermediate learners

The Gods of Japan

日本の神々

Abe Naobumi

安部直文

Michael Brase = translator

マイケル・ブレーズ＝訳

IBCパブリッシング

装　　幀＝見増 勇介、鈴木 茉弓(ym design)
イラスト＝テッド高橋

撮影協力＝神田神社(東京) *p.126, p.127, p.128, p.129, p.135, p.136, p.137*
写真協力＝西宮神社(兵庫) *p.198*、アフロ *p.184*

本書は2020年に弊社から刊行された対訳ニッポン双書『日本の神々』(安部直文著、マイケル・ブレーズ訳)を
再編集したものです。

About the *Read Real NIHONGO* Series

Reading Sets You Free

The difficulty of reading Japanese is perhaps the greatest obstacle to the speedy mastery of the language. A highly motivated English speaker who wants to make rapid progress in a major European language such as Spanish, French or German need only acquire a grasp of the grammar and a smattering of vocabulary to become able to at least attempt to read a book. Thanks to a common alphabet, they can instantly identify every word on the page, locate them in a dictionary, and figure out—more or less—what is going on.

With Japanese, however, *kanji* ideograms make it infinitely harder to make the jump from reading with guidance from a teacher to reading freely by oneself. The chasm dividing the short example sentences of textbooks from the more intellectually rewarding world of real-world books and articles can appear unbridgeable. Japanese—to borrow Nassim Taleb's phrase—is an "Extremistan" language. *Either* you master two thousand *kanji* characters with their various readings to achieve breakthrough reading proficiency and the capacity for self-study *or* you fail to memorize enough *kanji*, your morale collapses, and you retire, tired of floating in a limbo of semi-literacy. At a certain point, Japanese is all or nothing, win or lose, put up or shut up.

The benefits of staying the course and acquiring the ability to read independently are, of course, enormous.

Firstly, acquiring the ability to study by yourself without needing a teacher increases the absolute number of hours that you can study from "classroom time only" to "as long as you want." If there is any truth to the theories about 10,000 hours of practice being needed to master any skill, then clearly the ability to log more hours of Japanese self-study has got to be a major competitive advantage.

Secondly, exposure to longer texts means that your Japanese input rises in simple quantitative terms. More Japanese *going into* your head means that, necessarily, more Japanese *stays in* your head! As well as retaining more words and idioms, you will also start to develop greater mental stamina. You will get accustomed to digesting Japanese in real-life "adult" portions rather than the child-sized portions you were used to in the classroom.

Thirdly, reading will help you develop tolerance for complexity as you start using context to help you figure things out for yourself. When reading a book, the process goes something like this: You read a sentence; should you fail to understand it first time, you read it again. Should it still not make sense to you, you can go onto the next sentence and use the meaning of that one to "reverse-engineer" the meaning of its predecessor, and so on. By doing this, you will become self-reliant, pragmatic and—this is significant—able to put up with gaps in your understanding without panicking, because you know they are only temporary. You will morph into a woodsman of language, able to live off the land, however it may be.

That is the main purpose of the *Read Real NIHONGO* series: to propel you across the chasm that separates those who read Japanese from those who cannot.

Furigana the Equalizer

Bilingual books have been popular in Japan since the 1990s. Over time, they have grown more sophisticated, adding features like comprehensive page-by-page glossaries, illustrations and online audio. What makes the *Read Real NIHONGO* series—a relative latecomer to the scene—special?

It all comes down to *furigana*. This is the first ever series of bilingual books to include *furigana* superscript above every single *kanji* word in the text. Commonly used in children's books in Japan, *furigana* is a tried-and-tested, non-intrusive and efficient way to learn to read *kanji* ideograms. By enabling you to decipher every word immediately, *furigana* helps you grasp the meaning of whole passages faster without needing to get bogged down in fruitless and demoralizing searches for the pronunciation of individual words.

By providing you with the pronunciation, *furigana* also enables you to commit new words to memory right away (since we remember more by sound than by appearance), as well as giving you the wherewithal to look them up, should you want to go beyond the single usage example on the facing English page. *Read Real NIHONGO* provides a mini-glossary on each right page to help you identify and commit to memory the most important words and phrases.

Raw Materials for Conversation

So much for *furigana* and the language-learning aspect—now for the content. The books in this series are all about Japan, from its customs, traditions and cuisine to its history, politics and economy. Providing essential insights into what makes the Japanese and their society tick, every book can help you as you transition from ignorant outsider to informed insider. The information the books contain gives you a treasure trove of raw materials you can use in conversations with Japanese people. Whether you want to amaze your interlocutors with your knowledge of Japanese religion, impress your work colleagues with your mastery of party-seating etiquette and correct bowing angles, or enjoy a heated discussion of the relative merits of arranged marriages versus love marriages, *Read Real NIHONGO* is very much the gift that keeps on giving.

We are confident that this series will help everyone—from students to businesspeople and diplomats to tourists—start reading Japanese painlessly while also learning about Japanese culture. Enjoy!

Tom Christian
Editor-in-Chief
Read Real NIHONGO Series

まえがき

　新天皇（126代）が即位し、元号が「令和」と改まりました（2019年5月）。日本の元号の最初は「大化」（西暦645年制定）で、中国をまねた表記でした。中国では紀元前2世紀頃から元号を用いるようになり、最後の王朝・清の治世（1912年）までの2050年間に約500の元号が存在したとされます。一方、日本では「令和」を含めこれまで248の元号が用いられました。なお、一つの元号は天皇の在位中に限るとする「一世一元」は明治（1868年改元）以降の制度で、それ以前は大災難が起きたときなどに世の安寧を願って改元するということがしばしばおこなわれたのです。

　日本最古の史書とされる『古事記』（712年成立）には、初代の神武天皇から33代推古天皇（女帝）までの歴代天皇の名前が記されています。そして、2代綏靖天皇から9代開化天皇までは実在していなかった、系譜が確かなのは26代継体天皇（507年即位）から、などといわれてきました。とはいえ、仮に継体天皇以来としても約1500年の皇室史は、イギリス王室の約950年をはるかに超えて世界最長です。

　『古事記』は、日本の国土をつくったのも、天皇の先祖も「神」としています。ただし、この神はキリスト教やイスラム教のような唯一絶対神ではありません。日本神話には無数の神々が登場しますが、それらの多くは極めて「人間的」です。このことは、日本の神は人々の心が生み育ててきたという示唆を含んでいるといえるでしょう。そして、これらの神々は今も全国に約11万あるともされる神社に祀られています。本書の主眼は、日本人のアイデンティティに関わる神話の成り立ちや主な神々とそれを祀る神社を通じて、日本文化への深い理解をうながすことです。このたびの改元を機に、国内外を問わずより多くの方々に本書をひもといていただければ幸いです。

安部　直文

Preface

The current Japanese emperor (the 126th) ascended the throne in May 2019, and the era of his reign was named Reiwa (Beautiful Harmony). The first era name to appear in Japanese history was Taika, which was established in 645. The custom of assigning era names followed Chinese practice. In China, era names came into use around 2 BC and came to an end with the fall of the Qing dynasty in 1912. In a period spanning 2,050 years, about 500 era names had been put to use. In Japan, on the other hand, including Reiwa, there have been 248 era names. Further, the system of employing one era name for the reign of one emperor (*issei-ichigen*) was adopted in 1868 in the Meiji period. Previous to that, whenever there was a natural disaster or catastrophic event, the era name would often be changed during the reign of an emperor in the hope of fostering peace and stability.

The names of the emperors from the first (Jinmu) to the thirty-third (Empress Suiko) are recorded in the *Kojiki* (Records of Ancient Matters; compiled 712). The emperors from the second (Suizei) to the ninth (Kaika) are considered to be legendary rather than factual. The list of Japanese emperors is held to be reliable from the twenty-sixth emperor, Keitai (enthroned 507). Even in this case, however, the history of the Japanese imperial household is approximately 1,500 years old, making it much older than, say, the 950-year-old British royal family.

According to the *Kojiki*, the creator of the Japanese archipelago and the progenitor of the imperial line were gods (*kami*). However, this god or gods were not all-powerful monotheistic gods such as found in Christianity or Islam. In Japanese mythology there are an almost countless number of gods, but most of these gods are very human-like. This can be taken as a sign that the Japanese gods are a product of the Japanese heart or mind. Even now these gods are worshiped throughout the country in an estimated 110,000 shrines. It is the principal aim of the present book to foster a greater appreciation of the identity of the Japanese people by a study of the origins of its mythology and its principal deities, as well as the shrines where they are worshiped. By taking advantage of the recent instigation of the Reiwa era, it is hoped that people both at home and abroad will find this book a helping hand in understanding one aspect of the Japanese character.

Naobumi Abe

□即位する accede to the throne
□元号 era name
□表記 notation
□紀元前 BCE (Before the Common Era)
□清(清朝) Qing dynasty (Shīng cháo)
□治世 reign
□一世一元 one era name per reign
□安寧 peace and tranquility
□改元 era change
□史書 historical text
□系譜 genealogy
□唯一 unique
□無数の numerous
□人間的な human-like
□示唆を含んでいる suggest
□主眼 main goal
□本書をひもとく explore this book

目次

Contents

4章 代表的な神社 ·················· 157

東日本 ··················· 158

西日本 ··················· 178

Chapter 4 Representative Shrines ·········· *157*

East Japan ·········· *158*

West Japan ·········· *178*

●音声一括ダウンロード●

本書の日本語の朗読音声（MP3形式）を下記URLとQRコードから無料でPCなどに一括ダウンロードすることができます。

https://ibcpub.co.jp/audio_dl/0810/

※ダウンロードしたファイルはZIP形式で圧縮されていますので、解凍ソフトが必要です。

※MP3ファイルを再生するには、iTunes（Apple Music）やWindows Media Playerなどのアプリケーションが必要です。

※PCや端末、ソフトウェアの操作・再生方法については、編集部ではお答えできません。付属のマニュアルやインターネットの検索を利用するか、開発元にお問い合わせください。

Audio Download

You can download the audio version (MP3 format) of this book in Japanese to your PC or other devices free of charge from the following URL and QR code:

https://ibcpub.co.jp/audio_dl/0810/

Please note the following:

* The downloaded files are compressed in ZIP format, so decompression software is required.

* To play MP3 files, applications such as iTunes (Apple Music) or Windows Media Player are required.

* The editorial team cannot answer questions about PC, device, or software operation and playback methods. Please consult the provided manual, search online, or reach out to the developer.

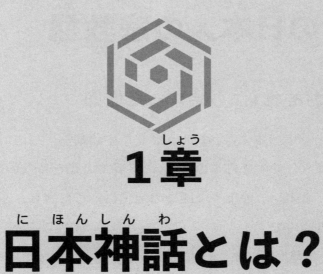

1章

日本神話とは？

Chapter 1

Japanese Mythology

§古代の日本人の宗教観

自然への「おそれ」から始まった信仰

　１万年以上も前の日本人は、狩猟や採集を生活基盤にしていました。いわば、**自然まかせの暮らし**です。日本の自然は、**世界でも類をみないほど四季の区別が**はっきりしています。このような四季の変化に応じた暮らしぶりが、古代から続く日本人の特質なのです。

　一方、日本は地震大国です。日本列島の中央部には**活火山が点々と分布し**、さらに列島下部にあるプレートの圧縮運動によるひずみが１億年以上も続き、これらが地震を頻発させてきました。2011年３月11日、東北地方太平洋沖でマグニチュード9.0の巨大地震が起き、大津波によって東日本沿岸に甚大な被害をもたらしました。この東日本大震災では、死者・行方不明者・災害関連死者の合計が2.2万人にものぼりました。さらに、大津波の冠水で過酷事故を起こした原子力発電所による被害もあわせ、日本での第二次世界大戦後最悪の自然災害とされます。

　2024年１月１日には、石川県能登地方でマグニチュード7.6の大地震が起き、５県での住家被害7.7万軒、８県での死傷者は1540人にのぼりました（令和6年能登半島地震被害状況：消防庁２月26日時点）。

　自然災害が起きるたびに日本人は、**自然の猛威**を思い知らされてきました。これは、古代も現代も変わりません。違っているのは、古代人は現代人のように予知や防災・減災といった備えをしようとしなかったことです。古代人にとって自然は、恵みをもたらすだけでなく災害をまねく「おそれるべきもの」でした。この「**おそれ**」には、**畏敬**と恐怖という両面の感情があり、それが自然への信仰に結びついたのです。

§ The Religious Views of Ancient Japanese

The Fear of Nature as the Genesis of Religion

More than 10,000 years ago the basis of life in Japan was hunting and gathering. In a sense, the people's lives were in the hands of nature. In fact, Japan is unequaled in the clarity of the distinction between the four seasons. Living in accordance with the changing seasons has been a special characteristic of Japanese life from ancient times until the present day.

On the other hand, Japan is a land of earthquakes. There are active volcanoes throughout the central area of the archipelago, and tectonic plates beneath the islands create pressures which have been causing slippage and frequent earthquakes for 100 million years. On March 11, 2011 a magnitude 9.0 earthquake off the coast of Tohoku caused a monstrous tsunami along the coast of Eastern Japan. 22,000 people were killed, went missing, or died of related causes due to the Great East Japan Earthquake. Combining this with severe accidents at nuclear power plants caused by the tsunami, the result was the greatest natural disaster in postwar Japan.

On January 1, 2024, a powerful 7.6 magnitude earthquake struck the Noto area in Ishikawa Prefecture. This devastating quake damaged 77,000 homes across five prefectures and resulted in 1,540 deaths in eight prefectures.

Every time a natural disaster occurs, Japanese are reminded of the terrible power of nature. This is as true today as it was in the past. The difference between now and then is that the ancients didn't have the means of prediction, protection, and moderation of disasters. For the ancients nature was not only a source of natural blessings but also a source of fearful catastrophe. This fear had two aspects—awe and fearfulness—and it is these two aspects that led to the worship of nature.

□生活基盤 lifeline
□自然まかせ at the mercy of nature
□世界でも類をみないほど unparalleled anywhere in the world
□変化に応じた in response to the change
□特質 distinguishing feature
□活火山 active volcano
□点々と分布する be scattered across the area
□圧縮運動によるひずみ strain caused by the compression
□頻発する occur frequently
□甚大な被害 extensive damage
□〜にものぼる amount to as much as
□冠水 flooding
□過酷事故 serious accident
□消防庁 Fire and Disaster Management Agency
□自然の猛威 destructive power of nature
□おそれ awe and fear
□畏敬 reverence

02

古代人と文明社会の自然観

　信仰の原初形態としてのアニミズムは、自然(生物・無機物)の中に精霊や霊魂をみるというものです。古代の日本人もアニミズムでしたが、これは奇しくも現代の日本が世界的な評価を得ているアニメーションという形で表出しています。アニミズムもアニメーションも、語源は「気息・霊魂」を意味するラテン語のアニマ(anima)です。アニメーションは静止画を連続させることで動画にする手法で、静止画がまるで魂を吹きこまれたように動くことから名づけられました。

　アニミズムという言葉は、19世紀後期にイギリスの人類学者E・B・タイラーが著書の中で使ったことで定着しましたが、彼はこれを文明社会の神概念とは異なる未開民族の精霊信仰と定義しました。その背景には、未開民族に対する偏見や蔑視が介在しています。そして、現代の文明社会に暮らす人々の宗教的価値観にも大きな影響を与えているのです。

　文明社会は、人間が自然を淘汰することで発展してきました。西洋の科学文明が流入した明治時代以降、日本人の自然観は次第に変容してゆきます。1923年9月1日に起きたマグニチュード7.9の巨大地震による関東大震災を体験、調査した物理学者の寺田寅彦は、急速に近代化して人口が密集した東京や横浜などの市街が無残な姿になったことにショックを受け、のちにこう書き記しています。「…文明が進めば進むほど天然の暴威による災害が劇烈の度を増す…中略…文明が進むに従って人間は次第に自然を征服しようとする野心を生じた」と。

Ancient Japanese and Modern Society's View of Nature

Animism, as the earliest form of religion, saw souls or spirits in nature, both in organic and in inorganic matter. Surprising enough, the animism practiced by ancient Japanese has found expression and worldwide recognition in the art form called "animation." The word itself derives from the Latin *anima*, meaning "breath" or "spirit." Animation is the technique of displaying still images in quick succession so that they appear to be moving. They seem to have been instilled with life.

The word "animism" was first used in the late 19th century by the English anthropologist Edward Tylor and thereafter became established. He defined animism as a spiritual religion of primitive peoples different from the concept of god held by modern societies. Lying behind this definition was a certain amount of bias and prejudice against primitive societies. Animism has also had a great influence on the religious values of people living in modern societies.

Civilized society developed by selecting the best nature had to offer. When Western civilization, based on scientific thinking, was introduced into Japan from the mid-19th century and thereafter, the Japanese view of nature underwent a gradual change. On September 1, 1923, a 7.9 magnitude earthquake struck Japan. This was the Great Kanto Earthquake. The physicist Torahiko Terada, who experienced the quake firsthand, was shocked when he saw, and later researched, the devastation that had been brought upon the rapidly modernizing and densely populated cities of Tokyo, Yokohama, and nearby areas. Later he wrote, "... the more civilization advances, the greater will be Nature's rage in the form of natural catastrophes.... As civilization advanced, man gradually developed the ambition to conquer Nature."

□ 原初形態 primordial form
□ 無機物 inorganic matter
□ 精霊 spirit
□ 霊魂 soul
□ 奇しくも coincidentally
□ 表出する manifest
□ 気息 aura
□ 静止画 still image
□ 魂を吹きこまれた be brought to life
□ 人類学者 anthropologist
□ 神概念 concept of deity
□ 未開民族 primitive people
□ 定義する define
□ 蔑視 contempt
□ 介在する intervene
□ 宗教的価値観 religious values
□ 淘汰する weed out
□ 次第に gradually
□ 変容する transform
□ 物理学者 physicist
□ 無惨な姿になる be devastater
□ 暴威 fury
□ 劇烈の度を増す intensify
□ 中略 ellipsis

1万年以上続いた「戦争のない時代」

　東日本大震災は、**自然を人間の意のままにしようとしてきた文明社会**が、その反動で自然の報復を受けたとも**解釈**されます。また、文明社会に対する自然の警告という意見もあります。これは、古代の日本人が自然に対して抱いた畏敬と恐怖という両面の「おそれ」を、現代の人々が**再認識**すべきということにほかなりません。

　およそ1万6500年前から3000年前まで続いたとされる**縄文時代**の人々は、人間のみならず動植物や道具類にも霊魂があるとしていたことが、**遺構の発掘調査**で判明しています。さらに、「霊魂は永遠に続く」と考えていたことを、多くの**出土品**が物語っているのです。自然の中に霊魂をみるという古代のアニミズムは、いわば「**原始宗教**」です。しかし、人間もまた自然の一部ということから考えると、文明社会の宗教よりも低級であるとは言いきれません。縄文時代は1万年以上続きましたが、発掘された多くの遺構や人骨は驚くべきことに戦争の**形跡**をとどめていないとされています。これは、縄文人が「他人から奪い取る」のではなく「自然から与えてもらう」という生き方だったからです。文明人は未開社会の人々を「**野蛮**」として**見くだす**傾向がありますが、戦争をする文明人のほうがよほど野蛮ではないかと思われます。

　古代の日本人の「他人から奪い取らない」という生き方が変質したのは、縄文時代の次の**弥生時代**からというのが定説です。というのは、弥生時代は海外からさまざまな民族が**移住**してきて、縄文人を淘汰したからでした。なかでも稲作の**伝播**によって**定住化**が進んだことが、古代日本の新紀元となりました。

Over 10,000 Years without "War"

The Great East Japan Earthquake can be interpreted as nature's response to modern man's attempt to manipulate nature to his liking. Or some see it as nature's warning to modern society. In any case, of the two aspects in which ancient Japanese viewed nature—awe and fear—it was fear that modern man was called upon to reconfirm.

In the Jomon period—that is, from about 16,500 years ago to 3,000 years ago—the Jomon people believed that plants, animals, and even tools possessed spirits or souls, as is clear from surviving excavation sites. Further, the many excavated objects tell us that these people believed that the soul had eternal life. This ancient animistic belief—that souls or spirits could be seen in nature—might be called primitive religion. However, since human beings are a part of nature, it is hard to say that this religion is of a lower level than the religions of modern society. The Jomon period continued for more than 10,000 years, but amazingly the many excavated artifacts and human remains show no traces of warfare. This is because the Jomon people lived lives based on receiving from nature, not of taking from others. Modern, civilized societies tend to look down on primitive peoples as being "barbarians," but in fact is it not war-loving modern man who is the barbarian?

It is generally thought that the ancient Jomon way of not taking from others underwent a transformation in the period that followed—the Yayoi period (300 BC–300 AD). It was then that many different peoples migrated to Japan and replaced the Jomon people through a process of natural selection. Among these people were those who, thanks to rice cultivation, took up a sedentary way of life. This marked a new epoch in the history of ancient Japan.

□ 自然を人間の意のままにする control nature
□ 反動 backlash
□ 報復 vengeance
□ 解釈される be open to interpretation
□ 警告 caution
□ 再認識する reaffirm
□ 縄文時代 Jomon period (16,500–3,000 years ago)
□ 遺構 remains
□ 発掘調査 archaeological excavation
□ 出土品 artifact
□ 原始宗教 primitive religion
□ 形跡をとどめる show traces of
□ 野蛮 barbaric
□ 見くだす look down on
□ 弥生時代 Yayoi period (300BC–300AD)
□ 移住する migrate
□ 伝播 spread
□ 定住 settle down

たくさんの神々がいる日本

　海を渡って日本にやってきた人々は、縄文人を驚かせる先進の技術や文物をもたらしました。北からは朝鮮半島を経て騎馬民族、南からは東南アジアの航海民、というように弥生時代の日本は先住民の縄文人と異民族との交流が盛んでした。

　このような交流を通して、縄文時代のアニミズムも変質してゆきます。やがて、たくさんの神々が創り出され、それぞれに物語ができました。これが、「神話」です。日本神話に登場する神々は、外国からやってきた神も含んでいて、極めて人間に近い存在として表現されています。一般に、宗教とは「人間の力や自然の力を超越した存在を中心とする観念」と定義されます。この「超越した存在」が、神というわけです。しかし、この説明はキリスト教、ユダヤ教、イスラム教などの「一神教」に対するもので、日本のような古代から続く「多神教」にはあてはまりません。

　例えば、日本には「捨てる神あれば拾う神あり」ということわざがあります。一神教の信者が唯一絶対神に見捨てられたなら永遠に救いはありませんが、多神教の世界では必ずどこかに救ってくれる神がいるというわけです。神と人間との関係が一神教のように厳格でないことが、良くも悪くも多神教の特徴です。

　古代日本の神々は、数えきれないほどたくさんという意味をもつ「八百万神」と総称されます。しかも、人格神だけでなく、山や滝などの自然や動植物などをも神としているのです。

Japan, a Land Teeming with Gods

These people who came to Japan across the waters brought with them many things, both technical and cultural, that amazed the Jomon inhabitants. There was a lively interchange between the indigenous Jomon and these newly arrived immigrants, which included mounted tribes from the north through the Korean peninsula and boat people from Southeast Asia.

It was through this type of interchange that Jomon animism was also transformed. Over time, a plethora of gods was created, each with its own story. This is what is meant by *shinwa* ("god story"), the Japanese word for "myth." Among the gods appearing in Japanese myths that came from abroad are some that are depicted in forms that are very human-like.

Religion is generally defined as "a concept that centers on a presence that transcends the powers of man and nature." However, this definition is applicable to the monotheistic religions of Christianity, Judaism, and Islam but not to the polytheism that has come down to us from ancient Japan.

For instance, there is the Japanese proverb "If you are abandoned by one god, you can be saved by another." In a monotheistic religion, if one is abandoned by the all-powerful, all-knowing God, one is abandoned forever, but in polytheism there is always a god somewhere who will come to your rescue. For better or worse, the relationship between gods and man is not as strict and unforgiving as it is in monotheistic religions.

In ancient Japan the number of gods was virtually uncountable, which was expressed by the phrase *yaoyorozu no kami* (literally, Eight Million Gods). These gods included not only those that took human form but also mountains, waterfalls, plants, and animals.

□文物 cultural artifacts
□騎馬民族 nomadic people
□航海民 seafarers
□先住民 indigenous people
□異民族 immigrants
□交流 interaction
□変質する change
□一般に generally
□超越した存在 transcendent being
□観念 concept
□一神教 monotheistic religion
□多神教 polytheism
□ことわざ proverb
□見捨てられる be abandoned
□厳格 strict
□良くも悪くも for better or worse
□総称される be called

稲作と祖霊崇拝

05

　縄文時代後期の推定人口は、20万人ほどとされます。それが次の弥生時代になると、3倍の60万人ほどに増えました。この人口増加をもたらしたのが稲の水田耕作で、それまでの狩猟や採集といった食料獲得の手段を大きく変化させると共に、人々の定住化を促進しました。野生の植物は、種子が熟すと地面に落とし、適度の休眠期間をへて発芽させますが、種子ごとに発芽時期を微妙にずらします。この遺伝的習性を人間に都合が良いように変えたのが栽培種で、5000年以上も前の縄文人はクリやマメなどの栽培をしていたことが判明しています。

　稲の栽培の歴史は7000年前にさかのぼるとされ、日本に栽培種が伝来したのは縄文時代後期ともいわれますが、水田耕作が主流になったのは弥生時代です。日本で稲作が普及したのは、気候風土が適していた、水が豊富、狭い土地でも生産性が高い、長期の保存が可能、などの理由からです。加えて、一定時期に大量に収穫できるように育種したことで、人口増加に応じられる食料確保が可能になりました。

　稲作によって古代人は食料を求めて遠出をする必要がなくなりましたが、ほぼ通年にわたる管理と多くの人手がかかります。そのため、水田の周辺に血がつながった一族が住んで結束したのです。そして、一族ごとに守護神を祀り、稲が無事に育ち、豊かな収穫が得られるように祈りました。これが、祖霊崇拝の起源です。

Rice Cultivation and Ancestor Worship

Near the end of the Jomon period the population of Japan was about 200,000 people. In the following Yayoi period it tripled to 600,000. What lay behind this tremendous increase was the cultivation of rice. It not only transformed the previous hunting and gathering means of livelihood but it also encouraged people to take up a more sedentary life. With wild plants, seeds ripen and fall to the ground, and after a period of dormancy begin to germinate. The dormancy period is slightly different for each seed. By taking advantage of these slight genetic differences, cultivated species were produced for human convenience. It has become clear that over 5,000 years ago the Jomon people were cultivating chestnuts and beans.

The growing of rice is said to have a history of some 7,000 years, and cultivated species of rice apparently came to Japan at the end of the Jomon period. It was in the succeeding Yayoi period that rice paddies became the main means of agricultural cultivation. The cultivation of rice spread in Japan because of the suitability of the climate, the plenitude of water, rice's high productivity despite small available land area, the long-term storage of rice, and so on. Moreover, by breeding plants for large harvests at fixed periods of time, it became possible to produce enough food to support an expanding population.

While rice cultivation freed ancient Japanese from the need to travel far and wide in search of food, it also required strict management and a large workforce throughout the year. This is the reason that rice fields were surrounded by blood-related clans living together in tightly knit groups. Each clan worshiped its own protective god and prayed to it for the safety of its fields and bountiful harvests. This is the origin of ancestor worship.

□推定人口 estimated population
□稲の水田耕作 rice paddy cultivation
□手段 method
□野生の wild
□熟す ripen
□休眠期間 dormant period
□発芽する germinate
□遺伝的習性 genetic predisposition
□栽培種 cultivated variety
□栽培 cultivation
□判明する be revealed
□伝来する be introduced
□普及する spread
□気候風土 climate and soil conditions
□水が豊富 abundant water
□生産性が高い high yield
□収穫 harvest
□育種 plant breeding
□稲作 rice cultivation
□遠出をする travel long distances
□通年にわたる throughout the year
□一族が結束する the family bonds together
□守護神 guardian deity
□祀る worship
□祖霊崇拝 ancestor worship
□起源 origin

§神話の成り立ち

06

渡来人が創った神話

　祖霊崇拝は、中国大陸や朝鮮半島から日本に**渡来した**人々が持ちこんだと考えられます。近年に発表された「**DNA解析による日本人の遺伝的特徴**」によると、九州では縄文人と弥生人の混血が進んでいる、本州では遺伝的に韓国人や中国人に近い、縄文系の遺伝的特徴はアイヌ民族と沖縄人に残っている、など**遺伝学上、弥生人が渡来人**とその子孫であるとしています。そして、先住民の縄文人の遺伝的特徴をもった人々が、**海を隔てた本州の北(北海道)と南(沖縄)**に存在することに大きな意味があるのです。

　それは、縄文人が弥生人に淘汰されたということにほかなりません。**前述の**ように、縄文人は「**他人から奪い取らない**」という生き方をしていました。つまり、「**所有**」という**概念**とは**無縁**の暮らしです。しかし、渡来人が持ちこんだ稲作が**促進**した**定住化**は、土地や生産物の所有を意味しただけでなく、それらをめぐる争いを引き起こすことになったのです。弥生時代を**代表する大規模集落・吉野ヶ里遺跡(佐賀県)**からは、首が切断された人骨が300体ほど発見されました。明らかに、戦争がおこなわれたことを物語っています。

　渡来人はまた、**青銅や鉄**といった**金属器**をもたらしました。青銅は主に**祭祀具**として、鉄は**農耕具や武具・武器**として使われました。なかでも**強固で鋭利な鉄**の武器は、戦争では有利です。こうして弥生時代の日本では渡来人の勢力が急速に拡大し、それとともに、祖霊崇拝の**延長線上**で神話が創られるようになりました。弥生人は自らのアイデンティティを、神話に**託そう**としたのでしょう。

§ The Genesis of Japanese Mythology

Myths Made by Immigrants

Ancestor worship was brought to Japan, it is thought, by immigrant groups from the Chinese mainland and the Korean peninsula. According to a recent paper titled "Genetic Characteristics of the Japanese People as Revealed by DNA Analysis," there was a good deal of interbreeding between Jomon and Yayoi peoples in Kyushu; and in Honshu, there are traces related to Korean and Chinese peoples; and Jomon-related genetic characteristics are particularly strong in the Ainu and Okinawan peoples. That is, the Yayoi people were the immigrant groups (*toraijin*) who came to Japan and their descendants. It is highly significant that peoples with the genetic characteristics of the indigenous Jomon should be living in the north (Hokkaido) and south (Okinawa) of sea-bound Honshu.

This can only mean that the Jomon were absorbed or replaced by the Yayoi people. As explained above, the Jomon followed a principle of life of not taking from others. In other words, their way of life was unconnected with the concept of possession. However, when sedentary living fostered by rice cultivation was brought by immigrant groups (*toraijin*) to Japan, this meant not only that land and goods became possessions, but that conflict arose regarding their ownership. From the large excavation at Yoshinogari in Saga prefecture, the most representative site of the Yayoi period, some 300 skeletons have been unearthed with their heads severed—unmistakable evidence of armed conflict.

The immigrant groups also brought with them bronze and iron technology. Bronze was principally used for ceremonial regalia, and iron for agricultural tools and armor and weapons. In particular, strong, sharp weapons made of iron were advantageous in times of conflict. Thus it was that in the Yayoi period the power of the immigrant groups rapidly expanded, and at the same time mythology was created that was based on ancestor worship. The Yayoi people strove to establish their own identity through the creation of myths.

□ 渡来する come to Japan
□ DNA解析 DNA Analysis
□ 遺伝的特徴 genetic characteristics
□ 混血 interbreeding
□ 遺伝学上 genetically
□ 渡来人 immigrants
□ 海を隔てた across the sea
□ 前述のように as mentioned above
□ 所有 ownership
□ 概念 concept
□ 無縁の unrelated to
□ 促進した facilitated
□ 代表する representiative
□ 大規模集落 large settlement
□ 青銅 bronze
□ 金属器 metalware
□ 祭祀具 ritual implements
□ 農耕具 agricultural tools
□ 強固な strong
□ 鋭利な sharp
□ 〜の延長線上で in line with
□ 託す entrust

07

文字がない時代の物語

　日本で文字が使われるようになったのは、3〜4世紀ごろとされます。その文字は中国の漢字で、5世紀ごろから人名や地名などの**固有名詞**を漢字にあてはめて表記するようになりました。しかし、漢字を読み書きできたのはごく一部の人々で、多くは**話し言葉**としての日本語を使っていたのです。

　文字がない時代の日本語の**痕跡**をとどめる事例の一つが、アイヌ語です。アイヌという**呼称**は「人間」を意味し、もともとは「自然」を意味するカムイに対する概念です。そして、カムイという言葉は、「カミ（神）」を想起させます。つまり、文字がない時代の日本人は、**恵み**をもたらすだけでなく災害をまねく「おそれるべき」存在や**現象**をカムイ（カミ）と呼んでいたとも考えられるのです。ただし、「カミ（神）」の**語源**については、さまざまな説が**提起されている**ことを付言しておかなければなりません。

　文字をもたないアイヌ民族は、「ユーカラ（ユカラ）」という**叙事詩**によって自然の神々の神話や英雄伝説を**口承**しました。口承とは、文字によらずに口伝えすることです。アイヌ民族を含む縄文人はもとより、文字がない時代の人々はたくさんの神の物語を創って、口承してきたのです。

　日本の先住民の縄文人と渡来人との混血によって弥生人が生まれた一方、日本列島の最北にいたアイヌ民族は混血することなく縄文人としての暮らしを続けていました。寒冷地なので稲作ができなかったことも、その理由の一つです。**ちなみに**、アイヌ民族の子孫は、21世紀初頭の調査によると北海道内に2万人以上いるとされます。

Storytelling in an Age without Writing

Writing came to be used in Japan sometime in the 3rd or 4th century. It came in the form of Chinese characters (what Japanese call *kanji*), and by the 5th century people's names, place names, and other proper nouns had begun to be expressed in kanji. However, the proportion of people who could read and write kanji was very small; most people used spoken Japanese as their means of communication.

One clue to the nature of the Japanese language before the introduction of writing is found in the Ainu language. The word *ainu* itself means "human being," and it originally stood in contrast to the Ainu concept of "nature"—*kamuy*. This word resembles the Japanese word for "god" (*kami*). Thus it is possible that, before writing came into use, ancient Japanese used *kamuy* to refer to natural phenomena that not only brought bountiful blessings but also awe-inspiring catastrophe and disaster. As to the etymology of the word *kamuy*, various theories have been proposed, which I will touch upon here.

Not having a written language, the Ainu orally passed down in sagas called *yukar* the myths of the gods of nature and legendary figures. "Orally" here, of course, means by word of mouth. Ancient peoples, including the Jomon and the Ainu, created many tales about the gods and passed them down orally to later generations.

While on the one hand the indigenous Jomon intermingled with immigrant groups to produce the Yayoi people, the Ainu living in far north Hokkaido did not undergo intermingling and continued the Jomon way of life. One reason for this was that they could not undertake rice cultivation in the cold northern climate. Incidentally, according to a poll taken at the beginning of the 21st century, the population of Ainu descendants in Hokkaido was over 20,000.

□固有名詞 proper noun
□あてはめる apply
□話し言葉 spoken language
□痕跡をとどめる leave traces
□事例 example
□呼称 name
□想起させる resemble
□恵み blessings
□現象 phenomenon
□語源 etymology
□提起される be raised
□付言する add
□叙事詩 epic poem
□口承する pass down orally
□口伝えする by word of mouth
□〜としての暮らし life as a 〜
□ちなみに By the way,

08

地神信仰から生まれた国神

　定住化が血縁共同体から地縁共同体へと拡大してゆくなかで生まれたのが、地神でした。これは、大地の神であり、穀物や豊穣の神であり、集落の守護神です。稲作が普及した弥生時代には、地神信仰が定着しました。やがて、土地をめぐる争いが各地で発生し、勝った共同体は広大な土地を支配しました。その過程で形成されたのが「国」で、最高権威者を「王」と呼んだのです。

　もっとも、これらの呼称は中国にならったもので、国といっても規模は中国とは比べものにならないほど小さく、弥生時代の一国の人口は数千単位ともいわれます。そして、これらの国々が領地をめぐって戦争を繰り返しました。古代人は、国の地霊を「国魂」と呼びました。戦いに負けた国は、勝者に国魂を渡すことで恭順を示したとされます。勝った国は、王を「国神」とする神話を創って後世に語り伝えたのです。

　記録にのこる古代日本の国として有名な邪馬台国は、女王が統治していました。女王は卑弥呼と呼ばれ、「日（太陽）の巫女」という意味だったとの説があります。巫女は、現代では神に仕える女性のことですが、古代には神の妻を意味していたとも考えられています。卑弥呼という名は、太陽神の妻をあらわしているのです。邪馬台国は2〜3世紀にかけて実在した国で、その国名から5世紀に成立した大和王権のもとになった国ではないかともされます。実は、3世紀と5世紀の間の100年余り、つまり4世紀は歴史上で「空白の世紀」ともいわれているのです。想像をたくましくすれば、この間、各地では国神を礼賛する神話が語り継がれていたのではないかと思われます。

Out of Worship of Land Gods (*Jigami*) Are Born Country Gods (*Kunitsukami*)

In the expansion of sedentary habitation from blood-related groups to regional-related groups, the land gods (*jigami*) were born. This was the god of bountiful land, the god of food grains and good harvests, the guardian gods of the community. With the spread of rice cultivation in the Yayoi period, the worship of the gods of the land became firmly established. Eventually, conflicts arose throughout the country over the ownership of land, and the victorious communities took possession of large expanses of territory. In the process of this development, "countries" (*kuni*) came into being, and their rulers were called *okimi* (kings).

Of course, such nomenclature was made in emulation of China. The "countries" were incomparably small in comparison to those in China. The population of a country in the Yayoi period is said to have been a matter of several thousands. These countries continually fought with one another over territory. Ancient Japanese thought of the spirit of the earth (*chirei*) as the soul of the country (*kunitama*). The defeated country is said to have relinquished its *kunitama* to the victors as a sign of allegiance. The victors would create a myth to be passed on to later generations in which their king would be designated a "country god" (*kunitsukami*).

The queen of the oldest Japanese country to be recorded in history was Himiko of Yamatai. She was a shaman (*miko*). The *hi* in Himiko, according to some theories, means the "sun," of which she was a shaman. *Miko*, in modern times, means a female who serves a god, but in ancient times it seems to have referred to the wife of a god. Thus "Himiko" can be taken to mean "Wife of the Sun God." The country over which she ruled, Yamatai, existed in the 3rd to 5th centuries. Judging from the similarities in names, it is speculated that Yamatai became the basis for the later Yamato imperial court. In reality, the intervening 100 years between the 3rd and 5th centuries—that is, the 4th century—is known, historically, as a "blank century." Left to our imagination, we can surmise that throughout Japan myths were being created during this period in praise of country gods (*kunitsukami*).

□血縁 blood ties
□共同体 community
□地縁 regional ties
□地神 local deities
□豊穣 bountiful harvests
□集落 settlement
□最高権威者 ruler
□〜にならった modeled after
□規模 size
□領地 territory
□地霊 earth spirit
□国魂 national spirit
□恭順を示す show obedience
□国神 country deity
□統治する rule
□巫女 shaman
□実在した existed
□空白 gap
□想像をたくましくすれば left to conjecture
□礼賛する exalt

「死と再生」のドラマ

　人類にとって最大の難問は、「死んだあと、どうなるのか？」といっても過言ではないでしょう。そして、この難問に対して、**それなりの答えを用意している**のが**宗教**なのです。多くの宗教は「死と再生（復活）」を最重要テーマにしていますが、古代の人々の暮らしはまさしくこのテーマを日常化したものでした。それは、「霊魂は永遠に続く」というアニミズムにもとづく「死と再生」の物語を創り出しました。この物語を壮大なスケールで表現したのが、国の支配層である王や豪族の墓、すなわち**古墳**でした。

　現在も日本の各地に点在する古墳は、約16万基。3世紀前半ごろから造られ始め、次第に巨大化して5世紀中ごろまでを**最盛期**としています。しかも、**前方後円墳**と呼ばれる巨大古墳は、日本独自の形をしているのです。古墳は巨大なほど、そこに埋葬された人物の権威の高さを示しています。巨大古墳が**集積している**のは奈良県や大阪府で、それよりも規模の小さいものが関東・北陸・九州などにのこっていることから、4世紀初めごろに成立した大和王権が、5世紀中ごろまでに地方豪族を従える形で国内の統一を進めていったと**推測されています**。

　大和王権の国内統一は、地方の国々との戦いの成果でした。**言い換えれば**、地方の国神を平定することで支配権を確立したのです。国神は**人格神**なので、人間と同様の感情をもつと古代人は考えました。戦いに負けた国神は、殺されるか**自害**しました。その**怨念**をもった霊（**怨霊**）をどうするかが、新たな**宗教的課題**になったのです。そのため、怨霊を再生（復活）できない別世界に**封じこめ**ようと考えました。弥生時代から**古墳時代**にかけての日本人は、「死と再生」についても独自の世界を創り出し、それを新たなドラマに仕立てたのです。

The Drama of "Death and Resurrection"

It is no exaggeration to say that one of the biggest questions mankind faces is, "What happens after death?" It is religion that tries to answer this question. Many religions take death and resurrection as their most central theme, and ancient peoples made that motif a part of their everyday lives. In fact, they created tales of death and rebirth based on the animistic belief that the soul of things had eternal life. Such tales were expressed on a magnificent scale in the construction of megalithic tombs of the aristocratic classes and kings—that is, of burial mounds or *kofun*.

Kofun, which can still be seen throughout Japan, were first built at the beginning of the 3rd century and reached a peak in size in the 5th century. They had a distinctive keyhole shape that is found only in Japan. The larger the *kofun*, the greater the power and authority of the person buried there. The large *kofun* are particularly concentrated in Nara and Osaka prefectures, with smaller ones found in Kanto, Hokuriku, and Kyushu. This leads one to believe that around the middle of the 5th century the Yamato imperial line had begun subjugating the powerful local clans and unifying the country.

The unification of the country under the Yamato court was the result of armed conflict with regional entities—that is, other "countries." In other words, by pacifying regional country gods (*kunitsukami*), overall sovereignty was established. Since these country gods were anthropomorphic, the ancients thought of them as having emotions like human beings. When they were defeated in battle, they were either killed or committed suicide. How to placate their vengeful spirits (*onryo*) became a problem with religious implications. The ancients' answer to this predicament was to confine these spirits to another world where they could not be resurrected or rise from the dead. From the Yayoi period into the Kofun period, Japanese created their own concept of death and resurrection, and from it they fashioned their own original drama.

□ 〜といっても過言ではない
It would be no exaggeration
to say that

□ それなりの答え a
reasonable explanation

□ 宗教 religion

□ 再生（復活） resurrection

□ テーマ theme

□ 日常化する become a part
of everyday life

□ 壮大なスケール
magnificent scale

□ 豪族 powerful clan

□ 古墳 burial mound

□ 日本の各地に点在する
scattered throughout Japan

□ 最盛期 peak

□ 前方後円墳 keyhole-
shaped *kofun*

□ 権威 authority

□ 集積している concentrated

□ 推測されている It has been
speculated that

□ 成果 result

□ 言い換えれば In other
words

□ 人格神 personal god

□ 自害する commit suicide

□ 怨念 grudge

□ 怨霊 vengeful spirits

□ 宗教的課題 religious
implications

□ 封じこめる confine

□ 古墳時代 Kofun period
(c.250–538)

大和王権の正当性を主張

5世紀中ごろの大和王権は「大王」を中心に、それを地方豪族が支えるという形で**中央集権化**を図っていました。そして大王は、のちに「スメラミコト＝天皇」と呼ばれるようになったのです。天皇という呼称は、中国の**道教**の影響を受けたものとも考えられています。さらに中国や朝鮮半島からは**儒教**や**仏教**が伝えられたことで、日本神話はさらに新たな**展開**を始めました。その**骨格**となったのが、「天神」の子孫である天皇が、「国神」である地方の王や豪族を**平定して統一国家を樹立した**、という神話の創作でした。

大和王権が中央集権化を達成したのは、7世紀末の天武天皇の時代とされます。それまでの間は、**王権内部での争い**が頻発するなど、不安定な王権時代が約170年にわたって続いたとされます。天武天皇は、クーデターによって皇位についた天皇ですが、即位後に天皇家に伝えられている系譜(**帝紀**)と伝承(**旧辞**)の誤りを正そうと、新たな**史誌作成**を命じました。これに関わったのが稗田阿礼で、記憶力が極めて優れた役人でした。しかし、天武天皇が亡くなったため、作業は**中断**してしまったのです。

「歴史は多くの場合、勝者の論理が優先される」ともいわれます。天武天皇も、おそらく自らの**正当性**も含めて大和王権の正当性を**確固**としたものにしておきたい、とのねらいがあったに違いありません。そして、その物語は天武天皇の死後26年後に『古事記』という書物としてまとめられました。ちなみに『古事記』は、**現存**する日本最古の歴史書とされています。

Promoting the Legitimacy of the Yamato Imperial Line

In around the middle of the 5th century, the Yamato imperial line that was centered on a "king" (*okimi*) attempted to establish a centralized government with the backing of powerful regional clans. Later *okimi* came to be referred to as *sumera mikoto* (great lord) and even later as *tenno* (emperor). The term *tenno* is thought to have arisen due to the influence of Chinese Daoism. Further influence from China and the Korean peninsula in the form of Confucianism and Buddhism gave rise to new developments in Japanese mythology. At the core of these myths was the story of how the emperor, who was considered a descendant of heavenly gods (*amatsukami*), pacified the regional kings and powerful clans, who were country gods (*kunitsukami*), and unified the nation.

The Yamato court is said to have succeeded in creating a centralized government at the end of the 7th century during the reign of Emperor Tenmu. Until then, there were frequent internal struggles for power within the court, and unrest continued for a period of 170 years. After Emperor Tenmu assumed the throne in a coup d'état, he ordered that a new historical work be compiled, correcting mistakes in the imperial genealogy and oral tradition. This was done under the direction of Hieda no Are, an official who was known for his extraordinary memory. Following the death of Tenmu, however, work on the project was discontinued.

It is often said, "History is written by the victors," and there is no doubt that Tenmu wanted to establish the legitimacy of the Yamato court as well as his own. His attempt to do this was brought to fruition twenty-six years after his death in the *Kojiki*, which is Japan's oldest extant historical work.

□ 大王 emperor
□ 中央集権化を図る centralizing power
□ 道教 Daoism
□ 儒教 Confucianism
□ 仏教 Buddhism
□ 展開 development
□ 骨格 foundation
□ 平定する pacify
□ 統一国家を樹立する unify the country
□ 王権内部での争い internal power struggles within the court
□ 帝紀 imperial records
□ 伝承 oral tradition
□ 旧辞 a Japanese history book that is thought to have existed before the *Kojiki* and *Nihonshoki*
□ 史誌 historical records
□ 正当性 legitimacy
□ 確固としたものにする establish
□ 現存する extant

§ 『記紀』神話

日本の成り立ちを語る『古事記』

　文字で著された日本神話は、『古事記』と『日本書紀』に代表されます。両書をあわせて『記紀』といいますが、いずれも1300年ほど前の大和王権が命じて創らせたものです。『古事記』は西暦712年に、『日本書紀』は720年に完成しました。

　『古事記』は序文と本文3巻から成り、上巻は神々の物語、中・下巻で初代の神武天皇から33代推古天皇までの系譜や事績が述べられています。**本文の冒頭で語られるのは、日本の成り立ちに関する「創成神話」**です。一神教では「初めに神が出現して、すべてを創造した」としていますが、日本神話では「天と地が分かれたところに神が出現した」とし、しかも「**次々と神が出現して、この世を形づくった**」と記しています。このような創成神話は、古代中国の陰陽五行思想の影響を受けたものです。

　そもそも大和王権の歴史書は、中国の史書の**模倣**でした。奈良時代の大和王権は、**律令**国家をめざしていました。律令とは古代国家の基本法を意味し、中国においては古い歴史をもっていたのです。『古事記』は漢字で書かれていますが、日本人が読みやすいように独自に工夫した「**日本漢文体**」で記されています。そのため、国内向けの歴史書として創られたとされるのです。

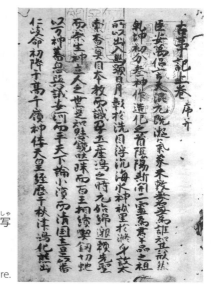

『古事記』写本（真福寺本）
現存する最古の写本。応安4年（西暦1371年）から同5年にかけて書写したもので、国宝になっている。愛知県宝生院蔵

A page from the Shinpukuji manuscript of the *Kojiki*.
The oldest extant copy. Produced in 1371 to 1372. Hosho-in, Aichi prefecture.

§ The Myths of the *Kojiki* and the *Nihon Shoki*

The Creation of Japan according to the *Kojiki*

The oldest written descriptions of Japanese mythology are the *Kojiki* (Records of Ancient Matters) and the *Nihon Shoki* (The Chronicles of Japan). They were both commissioned by the Yamato imperial court some 1,300 years ago. The *Kojiki* was completed in 712, the *Nihon Shoki* in 720.

The *Kojiki* consists of three main volumes with a preface. The first volume contains tales about the gods, and the second and third volumes narrate the genealogy and accomplishments of the first emperor (Jinmu) through the thirty-third emperor (Suiko). The first part of the text recounts the "creation myth" of how Japan came into being. Monotheistic religions begin with something like, "First there was God, who created all living things." In the Japanese creation myth, however, gods appear one after another at the point where heaven and earth divided and then create the world. This type of creation myth was influenced by the *yin* and *yang* philosophy of ancient China.

In essence, the histories compiled by the Yamato court were emulations of Chinese histories. In the Nara period (710–794) the Yamato court attempted to establish a system of administrative and criminal codes known as *ritsuryo kokka*. This referred to the basic law of the country, and it had a long history in China. The *Kojiki* is written in Chinese characters, but it is done in a form easy for Japanese to read called Sinico-Japanese (*Nihon kanbun-tai*). For that reason it is thought to have been written for a domestic readership.

□ 文字で著された written down
□ ～に代表される be represented by
□ 記紀 the *Kojiki* and the *Nihon Shoki*
□ 序文 preface
□ ～から成る consist of
□ 上巻 first volume
□ 中・下巻 second and third volumes
□ 事績 accomplishments
□ 本文の冒頭 the beginning of the text
□ 日本の成り立ち how Japan was formed
□ 創成神話 creation myth
□ 次々と in succession
□ 記している be recorded
□ 陰陽五行思想 *yin* and *yang* philosophy
□ ～の影響を受けた be influenced by
□ そもそも fundamentally
□ 模倣 imitation
□ 奈良時代 Nara period (710–794)
□ 律令 a system of administrative and criminal codes
□ 日本漢文体 Sinico-Japanese
□ そのため For that reason

12

天皇家の系譜を記す『日本書紀』

　『古事記』が国内向けとすると、『日本書紀』は国外向け、つまり中国を強く意識した歴史書といえます。『日本書紀』は全30巻から成り、1巻と2巻は神代紀、3巻以下は歴代天皇の事績を41代持統天皇に至るまで、漢字で詳述しています。全30巻というぼう大な分量になったのは、天皇の事績だけでなく、豪族や社寺の歴史、さまざまな神話や伝説、中国や朝鮮の資料が含まれているためです。また、これには系図1巻が付いていたとされますが、存在は不明です。

　『日本書紀』の3巻以下に登場する歴代天皇の初代は、神武天皇です。その名が示すように、神威を背景に武力で国内を統一したとされますが、以下25代までの天皇は不明な点も多く、実在したかどうかについては、さまざまな説があります。もっとも、『記紀』の編纂を命じた天武天皇 (西暦673–686年) は40代なので、その時点から遡ると1300年余もの時が経ったことになります。この間の天皇の系譜は、当然ながら漢字が導入される以前は記憶の所産ということなのです。

　一方、日本史で系譜が確かとされる天皇は26代継体天皇(西暦507–531年)以下、2019年5月即位の126代今上天皇までの101代で、これだけでも実に1500年余もの長遠な歴史を刻んでいます。天皇の系譜には、男系子孫が受け継ぐという「万世一系」の原則があります。このような原則を示した『日本書紀』の天皇の系譜は、それが事実かどうかはともかくとして、現代に至る日本史の前史として一考に値するものといっても過言ではないでしょう。

The *Nihon Shoki* and the Genealogy of the Imperial Family

If the *Kojiki* is directed toward a domestic audience, then it can be said that the *Nihon Shoki* is directed toward a foreign audience—that is, that it had China strongly in mind in its compilation. The *Nihon Shoki*, written in Chinese characters, consists of 30 volumes. The first and second volumes deal with mythological times. Volume 3 and the following volumes cover the achievements of historical emperors up to the 41st emperor, Jito. The reason the *Nihon Shoki* became such a huge tome is that not only does it cover the achievements of emperors, but it also describes the history of powerful clans, shrines and temples, recounts numerous myths and legends, and includes documents from China and Korea. There was also said to be a volume containing genealogical charts, but its existence is uncertain.

The first emperor to appear in the third volume and following volumes of the *Nihon Shoki* is Jinmu, who tops the list of all Japanese emperors. As his name (literally Divine Power) suggests he conquered the country through force of arms. There are many unclear points about the emperors that follow him up to and including the 25th emperor, and there are even various theories about whether these emperors actually existed. Of course, the emperor who commanded the compilation of the two histories was the 40th, Tenmu (r. 673–686), so the earliest events being related had taken place more than 1,300 years earlier. Thus the imperial genealogy of this time, before the introduction of a writing system, was a production of memory rather than the written word.

On the other hand, the imperial genealogy from the 26th emperor, Keitai (r. 507–531), to the 126th, the reigning emperor, who assumed the throne in May 2019, is unquestionable. This constitutes 101 generations and covers more than 1,500 years of history. The Japanese imperial genealogy follows the male line (called *bansei ikkei*), a principle established in the *Nihon Shoki*. Whether this genealogy is strictly true or not, it definitely deserves consideration as part of the prehistoric history of Japan leading up to the present.

☐ ～を強く意識した with a strong awareness of
☐ 神代紀 chronicles the age of the gods
☐ ～に至るまで up to and including
☐ 詳述している providing detailed accounts of
☐ ぼう大な分量 a massive amount of content
☐ 社寺 shrine and temple
☐ 伝説 legendary accounts
☐ 系図 genealogical chart
☐ 神威 divine power
☐ 編纂 compilation
☐ その時点から遡ると tracing back from that point
☐ 所産 product
☐ 一方 On the other hand
☐ 今上天皇 the reigning emperor
☐ 長遠な long-term and far-reaching
☐ 男系子孫 male lineage
☐ 万世一系 the unbroken male line of the Japanese imperial family
☐ 原則 principle
☐ 現代に至る leading up to the present day
☐ 前史 prehistory
☐ 一考に値する worth considering

「出雲神話」の背景

『古事記』で、神々の時代における重要な位置づけをされている話の一つが「出雲神話」です。ここでは、大和王権が地方豪族を従えたことが神話として語られています。出雲地方は日本海に面し、朝鮮半島に近いという立地から渡来人がたくさんやってきて、独自の発展をとげました。渡来人が移入したものの中に、鉄の製造技術があります。鉄は、武器や農工具として画期的な威力を発揮しました。これによって、出雲地方の豪族は強大な勢力を誇っていたのです。

　近畿地方に進出しようとした大和王権にとって、出雲地方を平定することは国内統一のうえで最大の課題でした。「出雲神話」は、平定後に大和王権によって創り出されたもので、天皇の正統性を補強する役割を担っています。前述（30ページ）のように、古代人の戦争では敗者が地霊である「国魂」を勝者に渡すことで恭順を示しました。そして、戦いに負けた国神（王）は殺されるか自害をしたのです。その怨霊を鎮めるために、出雲の国魂を大和王権の中に取りこんだのが「出雲神話」ということができます。

　出雲地方の国神の代表が、オオクニヌシ（大国主命）です。この国神は、天上界の主神アマテラス（天照大神）の弟スサノオ（須佐之男命）の子孫とされたことで、大和王権の系譜に連なります。そして、オオクニヌシが大活躍する物語を加えることで怨霊をなだめようとしたに違いありません。怨霊がこの世に現れて危害を加えないようにとの思いは、「霊魂は永遠に続く」と考えた古代人にとって切実な問題でした。「出雲神話」は、怨霊の鎮魂という意味合いを強くはらんでいるとも考えられます。

The Story behind the "Izumo Myth"

In the *Kojiki*, one of the important accounts that shows the position of the emperor in the Age of the Gods is the "Izumo Myth" (*Izumo shinwa*). In this myth it is related how the Yamato court brought powerful local clans under its sway. The Izumo region faces the Sea of Japan, and given the fact that it was not far from Korea, many people (*toraijin*) immigrated there, giving rise to their own distinctive culture. Among the various things they brought with them were the techniques for making iron. Iron-making, of course, was an epoch event in the manufacture of weapons and farming tools. Thanks to iron, the powerful local clans in the Izumo region wielded tremendous power.

For the Yamato court, which was attempting to invade the Kinki region, it was of ultimate importance to bring Izumo under its control and unify the country. The "Izumo Myth" was fabricated by the victorious Yamato court as a means of buttressing the legitimacy of the Yamato line. As mentioned on page 31, in war in ancient times the defeated party expressed its allegiance to the victor by surrendering the earth spirit of the land (*kunitama*) to the victors. The defeated country god (*kunitsukami*) was either killed or committed suicide. In the case of Izumo, in order to placate its vengeful spirit, the defeated spirit of the land (*kunitama*) was incorporated into the tale of the Yamato court as the "Myth of Izumo," as related in the *Kojiki*.

The most representative country god (*kunitsukami*) of the Izumo region is Okuninushi. Okuninushi was a descendant of Susanoo, the younger brother of the principal heavenly god, Amaterasu, and therefore connected genealogically to the Yamato court. By incorporation of a myth in which Okuninushi plays a active role, the aim was undoubtedly to placate his vengeful spirit. For ancient Japanese, who believed that the soul had eternal life, keeping vengeful spirits from appearing in this life and wrecking havoc was a crucial issue. The "Izumo Myth" also has strong undertones of a requiem for the dead.

□位置づけ positioning
□〜を従える bring 〜 under one's control
□面する face
□立地 location
□発展をとげる give rise to
□移入した introduced
□鉄の製造技術 iron-making techniques
□画期的な威力 groundbreaking power
□発揮する demonstrate
□強大な勢力を誇る wield tremendous power
□進出する invade
□最大の課題 ultimate importance
□〜によって創り出された be created by
□補強する役割を担う serve to reinforce
□〜に取り込む incorporate into
□代表 representative
□天上界の主神 principal heavenly god
□〜をなだめる placate
□違いない be undoubtedly true
□切実な問題 crucial issue
□鎮魂 requiem

「天孫降臨」が象徴するもの

　『記紀』では、天皇は高天原（天上界）の主神アマテラス（天照大神）の子孫であるとしています。それを示すのが「天孫降臨」の場面で、アマテラスの孫であるニニギ（邇邇芸命）が天上から降りてきて地上（葦原中国）の支配者になったとされます。このとき、ニニギは祖母のアマテラスから授かった三種の神器と稲を地上にもたらしました。三種の神器は、八咫鏡、八尺瓊勾玉、天叢雲剣（草薙剣）と呼ばれ、現在も皇室が継承しているとされます。

　古代人にとって鏡・勾玉・剣は高度技術の粋で、権威の象徴でした。また、稲作は新たな食料生産の手段というだけでなく、富の源泉となりました。そして、これらはいずれも渡来人が日本に持ちこんだものです。ちなみに古代の朝鮮半島には、天の神の子である檀君が地上に降りてきて、三種の宝器の呪力を用いて半島を統一したという神話があります。

　ニニギが降りたのは、日向（九州）の高千穂の峰とされます。この地名は、太陽神のアマテラスと稲の神であるニニギにゆかりがあることを示しています。古代の日本には、アジア一帯に見られる「穀霊信仰」がありました。なかでも稲作の普及とともに広まった「稲魂（霊）」への崇敬は、現代に至る神事の淵源です。古代人は、稲を生み出すとされる稲魂を山上で祀り、それを地上に降ろす儀式をおこなうことで豊作を祈ったのです。稲魂は雷神ともされ、雷光を「稲妻」と表記することにも、その関係性がうかがえます。『記紀』にはアジア各地の神話との共通点が多く見られ、「天孫降臨」もその影響を受けているという説もあります。

The Significance of the "Descent from Heaven"

According to the *Kojiki* and the *Nihon Shoki*, the Japanese emperor is the descendant of the principal god of the Plain of High Heaven (Takamagahara), Amaterasu. This is seen in the "Descent from Heaven" scene (*tenson korin*), in which Amaterasu's grandson, Ninigi, is sent down to earth (Ashihara no Nakatsukuni) to pacify Japan. It was then that the three celestial gifts and the rice ears that Ninigi and received from his grandmother were brought to earth. The three celestial gifts were the mirror Yata no Kagami, the sword Kusanagi, and the jewel Yasakani no Magatama. These three regalia are still said to be bequeathed to successive generations of the imperial family.

For the ancients, mirrors, jewels (*magatama*), and swords represented the essence of technological advancement and signified the ultimate in political power. Further, rice cultivation was not only a new means of garnering food but also a source of wealth. All of these were brought to Japan by immigrant groups (*toraijin*). Incidentally, there is a Korean myth that tells of Dangun, "the grandson of Heaven," descending to earth and pacifying the peninsula with the magical power of three kinds of treasured items.

Ninigi is said to have descended to the summit of Takachiho ("Thousand Rice Ears Heights") in Himuka ("Sun's Direction"; Kyushu). This place name indicates the connection between the sun goddess Amaterasu and the rice god Ninigi. The worship of the rice spirit (*Inadama*) seen throughout Asia is also be seen in Japan. In this, the veneration accorded the rice spirit that accompanied the spread of rice cultivation can be seen in the origin of the Shinto rites still practiced today. The ancients worshipped the rice-giving god on mountaintops and conducted rituals to bring the rice down to earth in plentiful harvests. This god was also known as the god of thunder and lightning, and "lightning" was written with the characters meaning Rice's Husband (*Inazuma*). There are many common points between Asian myths and the *Kojiki* and the *Nihon Shoki*, and some theorize that there is a strong Asian influence on the "Descent from Heaven" scene.

□天孫降臨 Descent of the Heavenly Grandchild

□場面 scene

□授かる receive

□三種の神器 the Three Sacred Treasures

□稲 rice ears

□〜が継承している be inherited by

□勾玉 *magatama* (comma-shaped beads)

□剣 sword

□高度技術の粋 pinnacle of technological innovation

□権威の象徴 symbolized the pinnacle of political authority

□〜だけでなく not only 〜 but also

□富の源泉 source of wealth

□呪力 magical power

□峰 summit

□ゆかりがある have a connection

□示す indicate

□アジア一帯 throughout Asia

□穀霊信仰 belief in the rice spirit

□稲魂(霊)への崇敬 veneration of the rice spirit

□神事の淵源 origin of Shinto rituals

□山上 mountaintop

□雷神 god of thunder and lightning

□雷光、稲妻 lightning

15

神武東征と大和王権の確立

　『記紀』に登場する神々の名や地名は漢字で書かれていますが、これらは日本語の当て字として使われているのです。例えば、初代の神武天皇は名をイワレヒコ(伊波礼毘古)と称し、天香具山の北東山麓の磐余という地名(現在の奈良県桜井市)に由来します。イワレヒコが初代天皇とされるのは、日向(九州)から瀬戸内海を経て大阪、熊野(和歌山)経由で大和(奈良)に入り、畝傍山の東南の橿原に建てた王宮で即位したという『古事記』の記述によります。そのプロセスを描写したのが「神武東征」神話で、アマテラス(天照大神)を祖神とする天皇家が、大和で王権を確立するまでの壮大な物語です。

　実は、天皇名は後世に諡号(おくり名)としてつけられたもので、この伝統は天皇の没後に在世中の元号を諡号とする形で現在に受け継がれています。さらに天皇名に神がつくのは、神武(初代)、崇神(10代)、応神(15代)の三人だけで、いずれも実在は不確かとされますが、『記紀』の「天孫降臨」を強調する意図があったためではないかと推測されます。「神武東征」は、天神が国神の上位にあるとすることで神々の序列化を進める根拠になったというべきでしょう。

The East Expedition of Emperor Jinmu and the Establishment of the Yamato Imperial Line

The names of the gods and place names that appear in the *Kojiki* and the *Nihon Shoki* were written in Chinese characters, but these characters were used to represent the sounds of Japanese rather than their Chinese meanings—a practice called *ateji*. For example, the personal name of the first emperor, Jinmu, was Iwarehiko. To write this in Chinese characters the name of an already existing place with the same pronunciation was used, which is now in present-day Sakurai city in Nara prefecture. How Iwarehiko became the first emperor is told in the "East Expedition of Emperor Jinmu" in the *Kojiki*, in which Iwarehiko travels from Himuka (Kyushu), along the Seto Inland Sea to Osaka and Kumano (Wakayama prefecture) and to Yamato (Nara). Here he erects a palace at Kashihara lying to the southeast on Mount Unebiyama and is enthroned. This grand myth tells the tale of how the Yamato clan, with Amaterasu as its guardian god, established the imperial line in Yamato.

Concerning the emperor's name, the fact is that the emperor was only assigned a name posthumously; before that, he was simply referred to as "the present emperor," a tradition that continues until today. Moreover, there are only three emperors whose names contain the character or word for *kami* (god or spirit): Jinmu (the first emperor), Suijin (the 10th), and Ojin (the 15th). The actual existence of these three emperors is questionable, and it is suspected that they were included to emphasize the legitimacy of the "Descent from Heaven" scene described in the *Kojiki* and *Nihon Shoki*. The intent of the "East Expedition of Emperor Jinmu" was undoubtedly to establish that the Heavenly Gods (Amatsukami) were ranked above the Country Gods (Kunitsukami).

□当て字 phonetic characters

□称する call

□由来する derived

□〜を経て、経由で via, through

□描写する describe

□祖神 ancestral deity

□諡号 posthumous name

□没後 posthumously

□〜とする形で in the form of

□現在に受け継がれている carried on to the present day

□〜の上位にある rank above

□序列 hierarchy

　近年、初期の大和王権の遺構として注目されているのが、三輪山麓の纏向遺跡(奈良県桜井市)です。ここには「箸墓」と呼ばれる国内最古の大型前方後円墳のほかに宮殿と見られる大型建物の遺構が存在しています。このことから、3世紀には大和王権がここを拠点にしていたとの説も有力です。それを前提にすれば、『記紀』が完成する8世紀初頭までの500年余りの大和王権の歴史は、「神話」という形で口承されてきたとも考えられます。

Recently the Makimuku excavation site at the base of Mount Miwa (Sakurai city, Nara prefecture) has received considerable attention as an old ruin of the early Yamato state. Here is found the oldest keyhole-shaped burial mound in Japan, called Hashi-haka, as well as the remains of a large building that appears to be a palace. This fact seems to bolster the theory that this area was the stronghold of the Yamato regime in the 3rd century. If this is true, then the 500 or more years of history until the *Kojiki* and *Nihon Shoki* were completed at the beginning of the 8th century can be said to have been passed down to later generations in the form of myths.

□拠点 stronghold
□有力 prevailing
□それを前提にすれば
　　Assuming this is the case

16

§日本神話の世界観

古代中国思想を反映した「創成神話」

「この世界はいつから始まったのか？」という問いは、古代人にも現代人にも共通のものでしょう。それを解明するために現代人は宇宙探査をおこなっていますが、古代人は神話の中にその解を示しました。

『古事記』の冒頭は、天地創成の場面から始まります。しかし、それは一神教のような万物の創造主がいるのではなく、「天と地が初めて姿を現し、やがて天に神々が出現した」というものです。この神々は、現れた順にアメノミナカヌシ（天之御中主神）、タカミムスヒ（高御産巣日神）、カミムスヒ（神産巣日神）という名で、「造化三神」とも呼ばれます。これらが現れたときの天地はまだ固まっていず、不安定でした。それを安定させるために出現したのが、ウマシアシカビヒコジ（宇摩志阿斯訶備比古遅神）、アメノトコタチ（天之常立神）、クニノトコタチ（国之常立神）といった神々です。

このように日本神話は天と地が未分化の状態を原初（世界の始まり）としていますが、これは古代中国の道教の影響を強く受けていると考えられます。この他に儒教・仏教・陰陽五行説などの思想が、6世紀までに日本に移入されました。なかでも天文術と易と五行論を核とする陰陽五行説は、この世界を読み解く神秘思想として大きな影響を与えたのです。大和王権は自らの正当性を裏付けるために、古代中国の世界観に基づく神話を創り出したというべきでしょう。

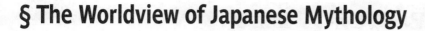

§ The Worldview of Japanese Mythology

The Creation Myth as a Reflection of Ancient Chinese Philosophy

Both ancient and modern man have asked the question, "When did the earth begin?" To answer this question modern man has explored outer space; ancient man indicated his answer in mythology.

The *Kojiki* opens with a depiction of the creation of heaven and earth. This is not, however, creation by an all-powerful monotheistic god, but rather it is described as follows: "In the beginning the heaven and earth appeared, and this was followed by the appearance of the gods." In order of appearance these gods were Amenominakanushi, Takamimusuhi, and Kamimusuhi—collectively called Zoka Sanshin (Three Gods of Creation). When these three gods appeared, heaven and earth were still unstable and unfixed. The three gods that appeared to bring stability to heaven and earth were Umashiashikabihikoji, Amenotokotachi, and Kuninotokotachi.

Thus, in Japanese mythology, heaven and earth were undifferentiated at the beginning of time. This view was most likely due to the strong influence of ancient Chinese Daoism. By the 6th century Confucianism, Buddhism, *yin/yang* and the Chinese doctrine of the five elements were also introduced into Japan. Among them, with astrology, divination, and the five elements at their core, astrology and the five elements played a significant role in explaining the world from an esoteric viewpoint. In the end, it can be said that the Yamato line attempted to validate its legitimacy through myths that were based on an ancient Chinese worldview.

□ 解明する elucidate
□ 宇宙探査 space exploration
□ 解 solution
□ 万物の創造主 Creator of all things
□ 造化三神 Three Gods of Creation
□ 出現する emerge
□ 未分化の undifferentiated
□ 原初 primordial
□ 天文術 astrology
□ 易 I Ching
□ 五行論 five elements theory
□ 核 essence
□ 神秘思想 esoteric thought

大和王権の支配地域を示す「国生み」

17

　『古事記』の天地創成に登場するのは17神で、先に現れた7神は**性別のない**独神、後に現れた10神が男女5組の神々です。その最後がイザナギ（伊邪那岐命）とイザナミ（伊邪那美命）という男女神で、高天原（天上界）から降りてきて、巨大な矛で地上を**かき回して**オノゴロ島を造りました。そして島で夫婦となって、さまざまな島や神を生み出したとされます。

　最初に生んだ島はアワジノホノサワケという名で、現在の淡路島です。次に生んだのがイヨノフタナという名の島で、この島は**四つの面**をもつとされます。その面はそれぞれ、男神名のイヨリヒコとタケヨリワケ、女神名のエヒメとオオゲツヒメと呼ばれ、現在の四国四県（香川・愛媛・徳島・高知）の元になった国です。やがて、大小14の島々からなる大八島国が誕生しました。これらは佐渡島（新潟県）以外は**近畿以西**（西日本）であることから、大和王権の支配地域を示す比喩ともいえます。

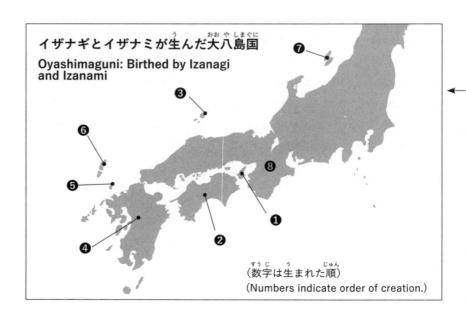

イザナギとイザナミが生んだ大八島国
Oyashimaguni: Birthed by Izanagi and Izanami

（数字は生まれた順）
(Numbers indicate order of creation.)

Areas in which the Yamato Regime Exercised Dominance

In the *Kojiki*, there are seventeen gods that appear at the time of the creation of heaven and earth, the first seven of which are without sex or spouse. The succeeding ten are man and wife pairs. The final pair is Izanagi and Izanami, who descend from the Plain of High Heaven to earth, where Izanagi dips a huge spear into the primordial waters and creates the island of Onogoro. It is here that Izanagi and Izanami are joined in marriage and create numerous islands and gods.

The first of the islands to be given birth to was Awajino-honosawake, which is present-day Awaji Island. The next was Iyonofutana, which was said to have consisted of four areas, two of which had the masculine names of Iyorihiko and Takeyoriwake, and two of which had the feminine names of Ehime and Ogetsuhime. These four now make up four prefectures in Shikoku: Kagawa, Ehime, Tokushima, and Kochi. Eventually, Oyashimaguni appeared, consisting of 14 large and small islands. Since all of these places, aside from Sado Island in Niigata prefecture, existed in the Kinki region or further west (West Japan), we may take this myth as an allegory of the area in which the Yamato regime exercised dominance.

□天地創成　creation of heaven and earth

□性別のない　genderless

□矛　spear

□かき回す　stir up

□四つの面　four sides

□近畿以西　Kinki region or further west

□比喩　allegory

---

❶ 淡路野穂之狭別島（現在の淡路島）

❷ 伊予之二名島（現在の四国）

❸ 隠岐之三子島（現在の隠岐島）

❹ 筑紫島（現在の九州）

❺ 伊伎島（現在の壱岐島）

❻ 津島（現在の対馬）

❼ 佐渡島（現在も同じ）

❽ 大倭 豊秋津島（現在の近畿地方）

❶ Awajinohonosawakenoshima (present Awaji Island)

❷ Iyonofutananoshima (present-day Shikoku)

❸ Okinomitsugonoshima (present-day Oki Islands)

❹ Tsukushinoshima (present-day Kyushu)

❺ Ikinoshima (present-day Iki Island)

❻ Tsushima (present-day Tsushima Island)

❼ Sadonoshima (present-day Sado Island)

❽ Oyamatotoyoakitsushima (present-day Kinki region)

18

生者を拒絶する「異界」

　イザナギ（伊邪那岐命）とイザナミ（伊邪那美命）は「国生み」を終えると、次に「神生み」にとりかかりました。生まれたのは35神とされ、**自然現象**、住居、穀物、船など**に関する**神々でした。これらは、古代人の暮らしを支えたものの**表象**とみることができます。

　しかし、「神生み」には、もう一つ重要な点が**記述**されています。それは、イザナミが火の神カグツチ（迦具土神）を産み、火傷が原因で死んでしまったことです。そして、イザナミは**黄泉国**へ去ってしまいます。その死を嘆き悲しんだイザナギは黄泉国に行き、妻に戻るようにうながしますが、願いはかないませんでした。

　前述（32ページ）のように、古代の日本人は「死と再生（復活）」について独自の世界観をもっていました。それを**象徴する**のが死の世界である黄泉国の**存在**で、**生者を拒絶する**「**異界**」です。**逆の見方**をすれば、死者が再生（復活）しないように「異界」に封じこめようとの、古代人の**宗教的心象の表れ**とも考えられます。

　黄泉国から逃げ帰ってきたイザナギは、死の世界の「**穢れ**」を**払う**ために川で「**禊ぎ**」をします。このときに生まれた15神の中に、アマテラス（天照大神）とスサノオ（須佐之男命）がいます。そして、イザナギは娘のアマテラスに高天原（天上界）を、息子のスサノオには大海を**治める**ようにとの**役割**を与えました。ところが、スサノオは「母親（イザナミ）がいる国へ行きたい」とごねたため、怒ったイザナギに**追放**されます。やがて神話は、この姉弟2神を中心にドラマチックに展開してゆくのです。

The Underworld's Rejection of the Living

When Izanagi and Izanami had finished giving birth to the land (*kuniumi*), they next undertook the birth of the gods (*kamiumi*). The 35 gods that were born were associated with natural phenomena, habitats, rice and grain, boats, et cetera. These can be thought of as symbolic of the things that supported the lives of ancient Japanese.

However, in the description of the creation of the gods there was one particularly important episode. When Izanami gave birth to the god of fire, Kagutsuchi, she died of injuries caused by the flames and departed for the land of the dead (Yominokuni). Devastated by Izanami's death, Izanagi followed her to Yominokuni and pleaded with her to return with him to the land of the living, but his pleas were in vain.

As mentioned above on page 33, ancient Japanese had their own original view of death and resurrection. This is represented by the existence of the land of the dead, Yominokuni, an underworld that rejected the living. To put this in another way, the attempt to confine the dead to the underworld, and to prevent them from reappearing in the world of the living, was one manifestation of the religious vision of ancient Japanese.

Escaping from the land of the dead, Izanagi purified his body with ablutions at a river to rid his body of underworld defilements (*kegare*). Among the 15 gods given birth at this time were Amaterasu and Susanoo. Izanagi gave his daughter, Amaterasu, the Plain of High Heaven to govern, and his son, Susanoo, the Sea. When Susanoo insisted on visiting the country where his mother lived, Izanagi became angry and expelled him. Hereafter a dramatic tale unfolds, based on these two siblings.

□国生み creation of the land
□神生み the birth of the gods
□自然現象 natural phenomena
□〜に関する be related to
□表象 representation of
□記述 account
□〜が原因で due to
□黄泉国 land of the dead
□象徴する symbolize
□生者 the living
□拒絶する refuse
□異界 underworld
□逆の見方をすれば Alternatively
□宗教的心象の表れ manifestation of religious beliefs
□穢れ impurity
□払う purify
□禊ぎ purification ritual
□治める rule
□役割 role
□ごねる insist on
□追放する expel

19

日本神道の「聖典」とされる『記紀』

アマテラス(天照大神)とスサノオ(須佐之男命)のエピソードは、2章(60ページ〜)で紹介します。ここでは、この姉弟神が日本神話の中で、どのように位置づけられているかについて少し触れておきます。

まずアマテラスですが、この女神はその名前が示すように太陽を象徴し、高天原(天上界)の神々の頂点に立つ最高神で、天皇家の祖神とされます。一方、スサノオは天上界から追放されたのちに地上に降りて出雲国の祖神となり、やがて根の堅州国という「異界」の支配神になります。このことから、アマテラスとスサノオは、「天上界」と「異界」を、大和王権と出雲国を、それぞれ代表する神として位置づけられていることがわかるのです。

実は、『古事記』と『日本書紀』が記述する神話がすべて共通しているわけではありません。とりわけ『古事記』で重要な位置を占めている「出雲神話」を、『日本書紀』はその大半を無視しています。『日本書紀』が大和王権の正史として編纂されたことを考えると、40ページで記したように大和王権にとって不都合な理由があったと考えるべきでしょう。その点、『古事記』の神話に登場する神々は喜怒哀楽が激しく、極めて人間的です。一神教が神と人間とを厳格に立て分けているのと違い、多神教は神と人間社会が混在する世界観を特徴としています。

とはいえ、『記紀』に登場する神々は、現代にあっても信仰の対象とされています。その意味では、ユダヤ教やキリスト教が『聖書』を「聖典」としているように、日本神道における「聖典」は『記紀』であるといっても過言ではありません。

The Two "Sacred Texts" of Shinto: *Kojiki* and *Nihon Shoki*

Various episodes in the lives of Amaterasu and Susanoo will be taken up in Chapter 2 (page 61 and thereafter). Here I would like to touch upon the position that these brother and sister deities occupy in Japanese mythology.

First, Amaterasu Omikami (Great August Deity Who Shines in Heaven). As indicated by her full name, she represents the sun and stands at the apex of the gods of the Plain of High Heaven as the guardian god of the imperial household. As for Susanoo, after he was banished from the Plain of High Heaven, he descended to earth and became the guardian god of the Izumo region, and later the governing force in the faraway underworld called Ne no Katasunokuni. From this it can be understood how the Yamato imperial line and the Izumo line of gods became representative of two different realms, one of the heavenly world and the other of the underworld.

If the truth be known, the tales told in the *Kojiki* and *Nihon Shoki* are not always consistent. In particular, whereas the "myth of Izumo" holds an important place in the *Kojiki*, over half of the myth is ignored in the *Nihon Shoki*. Considering that the *Kojiki* was meant to be the authorized history of the Yamato court, there must have been some inconvenient reason for this excision, as mentioned on page 41. In that respect, the gods appearing in the *Kojiki* are very human-like in their expression of strong emotions. In contrast to monotheism, which makes a clear distinction between god and man, polytheism is characterized by a worldview in which gods and human society are merged together.

Still, even today the gods that appear in the *Kojiki* and *Nihon Shoki* remain objects of worship. In that sense, just as Jews and Christians take the Bible as their sacred text, the sacred texts of Shinto can be said, without exaggeration, to be the *Kojiki* and *Nihon Shoki*.

□ 〜の頂点に立つ at the pinnacle of
□ 支配神 ruling deity
□ 共通している consistent with
□ 無視する disregard
□ 正史 official history
□ 編纂された be compiled
□ 不都合な理由 inconvenient reason
□ その点 In that respect
□ 喜怒哀楽が激しい expressive emotions
□ 厳格に立て分けている clear distinction
□ 混在する coexist
□ 信仰の対象 object of worship
□ 聖典 sacred text

20

古代人の想像力の所産

　日本神話の世界は、天上界と地上界、そして異界という三重構造になっています。天上界は「天神」が住み、地上界は「国神」と人間が住む世界です。一方、異界は地下や海底や海の彼方の世界で、「黄泉国」「根の堅州国」「海の国」「常世国」「夜の国」などと呼ばれる国々があります。

　しかし、これらの国々は厳密に区別されているわけでなく、どこにあるのかは不明です。

　実は、不明という点に異界たるゆえんがあるともいえます。古代人は見えない世界を「異界」として、想像力を働かせたと考えられるからです。

天上界
The Heavenly Realm

神々が生まれる前からあった世界で、「高天原」と呼ばれる。最高神はアマテラス（天照大神）という女神で、天皇家の祖神とされる。

This is the realm that existed before the appearance of the gods; it is called Takamagahara (Plain of High Heaven). Its chief god is the goddess Amaterasu, who is the guardian god of the imperial family.

地上界
The Earthly Realm

天上界から追放されたアマテラスの弟スサノオ（須佐之男命）が降りた地で、「葦原中国」とも呼ばれる。日本の国土と考えられている。

This is the earth to which Susanoo, the younger brother of Amaterasu, descended after being banished from the Plain of High Heaven; it is also known as Ashihara no Nakatsukuni (Central Land of Reed Plains). It is thought to refer to the territory of Japan.

A Product of Ancient Imagination

The world of Japanese mythology consists of three realms: the realm where the heavenly gods (*amatsukami*) live and the realm where the country gods (*kunitsukami*) and human beings live. The third realm (*ikai*) is underground, under the sea, or far over the ocean, and called by various names, such as Yominokuni, Ne no Katasunokuni, Uminokuni, Tokoyonokuni, and Yorunokuni.

However, these realms are not clearly distinguished; even their locations are unknown.

Actually, there is a possible reason that the location of the underworld is unknown. By designating this world as unknown, it can be said that the ancients left room for their imaginations to work.

□三重構造 three-layered structure

□彼方 the otherworld

□常世国 the land of perpetual life and eternal youth

□厳密に区別されている わけでなく not strictly separated

□〜たるゆえんがある there is a reason for

□想像力 imagination

異 界　　*Ikai*

黄泉国 *Yominokuni*　　死の国。この国の食べ物を口にすると、神も死者の姿になる。

Shinokuni: This is the land of the dead. By eating the food of this land, even gods are transformed into the forms of the deceased.

常世国 *Tokoyonokuni*　　海の彼方にあり、不老不死の国。地上界との交流がある。

Far across the sea, this is the land of perpetual life and eternal youth. It has communications with the earthly realm.

夜の国 *Yorunokuni*　　アマテラスのもう一人の弟ツクヨミ（月読命）が支配する国。

This is an earthly realm ruled by Tsukuyomi, a younger brother of Amaterasu.

2章

神々と英雄の物語

Chapter 2

The Gods and Heroic Tales

［1］アマテラスとスサノオ

「三貴子」の誕生

『古事記』の記述によると、黄泉国（死者の国）から逃げ帰ったイザナギ（伊邪那岐命）が「穢れ」を払うために川で身を清めたとき、15神が生まれたとされます。そして、左目を洗うと女神アマテラス（天照大神）が、右目を洗うと男神ツクヨミ（月読命）が、鼻を洗うと男神スサノオ（須佐之男命）が生まれました。これらの姉弟神は「三貴子」と呼ばれ、神々の中で特別な役目を与えられたのです。

太陽を象徴する名前のアマテラスは、天上界（高天原）の支配神という立場です。ツクヨミは、文字通り夜の国の支配神です。一方、スサノオはイザナギから海の支配神という役目を与えられましたが、それを拒否したため追放されてしまいます。そして、姉に別れを告げるために高天原にやってくるところから、新たなドラマが始まるのです。

スサノオを怖れたアマテラス

スサノオが高天原にやってくるときに国土が震動したため、アマテラスは「自分に代わって支配者になろうとしているのではないか」と疑念を抱きます。そこで、武装をして待ち受けました。スサノオは「お別れを言いにきただけです」と弁明します。アマテラスは、弟の本心をさぐるために「誓約」と呼ばれる占いを提案します。アマテラスの髪飾りの勾玉から生まれたのが5柱の男神、スサノオの剣から生まれたのが3柱の女神でした。スサノオの持ち物から女神が生まれたことで、邪心がないと証明されたのです。

しかし、その後がいけません。調子に乗ったスサノオは、高天原で乱暴狼藉を働いてしまいます。弟の暴挙を怖れたアマテラスは、岩窟に身を隠しました。

[1] Amaterasu and Susanoo

Birth of the Three Noble Children

According to the *Kojiki*, when Izanagi stopped by a river on his way back from the land of the dead, 15 gods were created when he purified his body from defilement. And then when he washed his left eye, the goddess Amaterasu was born; and when his right eye, the god Tsukuyomi; and his nose, Susanoo. These sibling gods were called the Sankishi (Three Noble Children) and were given special roles to play among the gods.

Amaterasu, as indicated by her full name (Great August Deity Who Shines in Heaven), was the chief deity in the Plain of High Heaven. Tsukuyomi, the moon god, was god of the night. Susanoo was appointed by Izanagi to rule the sea, but when he refused the appointment, he was banished from heaven. When he visited the Plain of High Heaven to say goodbye to his sister, Amaterasu, a new drama began to unfold.

Amaterasu's Fear of Susanoo

When Susanoo came to the Plain of High Heaven, Amaterasu felt the earth quake and suspected that Susanoo "had come to replace her as the ruler of the Plain of High Heaven." She donned armor and waited his arrival. Susanoo explained the reason for his coming by saying, "I have only come to say goodbye." In order to discover what Susanoo was really thinking, Amaterasu proposed that they vie in a type of fortune telling called *ukei*. As a result of this, five males gods were born from Amaterasu's bejeweled hair ornament and three female gods from Susanoo's sword. Since the feminine gods were born from Susanoo's possessions, this was considered proof that he bore no evil intent.

What followed, however, was unforgivable. Susanoo ran completely amuck. Frightened by her brother's violent behavior, Amaterasu took refuge in a rock cave known as the Ame no Iwaya.

□三貴子 Three Noble Children
□立場 position
□文字通り literally
□別れを告げる say goodbye
□国土 land
□震動する tremble
□疑念を抱く suspect
□弁明する explain
□本心 true intention
□誓約 oath
□占い divination technique
□邪心 evil intent
□調子に乗った overzealous
□乱暴狼藉を働く run riot
□暴挙 outrage
□岩窟 rock cave

22

アマテラスの誘い出し作戦

太陽神アマテラスが「天の岩屋」という岩窟に身を隠したため、天上(高天原)も地上(葦原中国)も暗闇になってしまいました。夜が続き、災いが起きたため、困り果てた神々は「安の河原」に集まって、知恵者のオモイカネ(思兼神)に打開策を考えるように依頼します。

オモイカネはまず、「常世国」(異界)から長鳴鳥を呼び集めて鳴かせました。日の出とともに鳴く鳥の声を聞かせることで、アマテラスを誘い出そうとしたのです。さらに鏡や勾玉などをつくらせて枝に掛け、アメノコヤネ(天児屋根命)にアマテラスをほめたたえる言葉(祝詞)を唱えさせました。そして、岩屋の戸の陰に腕力が強いアメノタジカラオ(天手力男命)を潜ませ、戸の前で女神アメノウズメ(天宇受売命)が破廉恥な踊りを披露すると神々は大笑いしました。

鏡に映った自分の姿に驚く

外が騒がしいので、アマテラスは岩屋の戸を少し開けて「私が姿を隠したことで天地は闇になったはずなのに、なぜ皆は楽しそうなのか」と問いかけました。すると、「あなたよりも尊い神がいらっしゃっているのですよ。ほら、この方です」という声とともに鏡が差し出されました。鏡の中の神の姿(実は、自分の姿)をよく見ようと岩屋から出た瞬間、戸の陰に隠れていたアメノタジカラオがアマテラスの手を引っ張り外に連れ出します。同時に、フトダマ(布刀玉命)が岩屋に「しめ縄」をかけて、アマテラスが二度と中に入れないように封印したのです。このように神々の連携プレーでアマテラスは姿を現し、天地は明るさを取り戻しました。

天上界の最高神がいとも簡単に騙されるところに、日本神話ならではのユニークな視点があるといえるでしょう。

The Strategy for Enticing Amaterasu Out of the Rock Cave

Once Amaterasu, the sun goddess, had hidden herself in the rock cave, both heaven (the Plain of High Heaven) and the earth (Central Land of Reed Plains) were thrown into total darkness. Night succeeded night, and disasters arose. The gods, thrown into consternation, gathered at Ama no Yasukawara and requested the wise man Omoikane to find a solution.

First of all, Omoikane assembled a number of long-crowing cocks from the underworld called Tokoyonokuni and had them crow. He hoped to entice Amaterasu out of the cave when she heard the sound of these birds which usually crowed with the rising of the sun. A mirror and jewel were made and hung on branches, and the god Amenokoyane sang a traditional chant in praise of Amaterasu. The powerful god Amenotajikarao concealed himself in a shadow of the cave, and the goddess Amenouzume danced a ribald dance, causing the other gods to roar with laughter.

Amaterasu Is Surprised at Seeing Her Own Reflection in the Mirror

Hearing all the clamor going on outside, Amaterasu asked, "Since I've hidden myself in the cave, heaven and earth should be pitch-dark. Why then is everyone seeming to have such a good time?" A voice answered, "Because a god greater than you has come. Look here and see." Simultaneously a mirror was held up for her to see. Hoping to get a better view of the god in the mirror (which was, of course, herself), she took a step out of the cave, and in that instant Amenotajikarao, who was hidden in a shadow at the entrance to the cave, grabbed her by the hand and pulled her out. Immediately the god Futodama lashed the entrance to the cave shut with with a sacred *shimenawa* rope to prevent Amaterasu from going back inside. This is how, through well-executed team play, Amaterasu was made to appear once again, and heaven and earth became bright once more.

In this depiction of how the principal heavenly god was so easily tricked, we can see what is one of the unique aspects of Japanese mythology.

□ 暗闇 utter darkness
□ 災いが起きる disasters occur
□ 困り果てた thrown into a state of despair
□ 知恵者 wise person
□ 打開策 solution
□ 長鳴鳥 long-crowing rooster
□ 祝詞 congratulatory words
□ 潜ませる concealed
□ 破廉恥な ribald
□ 尊い precious
□ しめ縄 sacred *shimenawa* rope
□ 封印する seal
□ 連携プレー well-executed team play
□ ～ならではの unique to this/that

天上界からも追放されたスサノオ

　アマテラスの復活後、騒動の原因をつくったスサノオに対して神々は、罰としてさまざまな品物を**献上させ**、身を清めさせるために長い髭や爪を切ったうえで高天原から追放します。スサノオは、父神(イザナギ)にも姉神(アマテラス)にも見放され、**放浪の旅**に出ることになってしまいました。

　ところで、「天の岩屋」の出来事は、**現代にも受け継がれている神事の原点**になっています。岩屋を封印した「しめ縄」、ご神体を映す「鏡」、神主が唱える「祝詞」、巫女が神に捧げる「舞」など、『古事記』の記述が**再現**されているのです。

Susanoo Is Banished from Heaven

After the reappearance of Amaterasu, as punishment the gods had Susanoo make a presentation of various offerings and cut his hair and fingernails as a form of purification. Then they banned him from the Plain of High Heaven. Abandoned by his father (Izanagi) and his older sister (Amaterasu), he could do nothing but take up the life of a lonely wanderer.

Incidentally, the episode at the rock cave is still alive today and forms one of the focal points of religious ritual. The sacred rope used to enclose the rock cave entrance, the mirror that reflects the image of the object of worship, the prayers chanted by the Shinto priests, and the shrine maidens who dance for the gods—all of this is a re-creation of the *Kojiki*.

□献上させる have someone make an offering

□放浪の旅 journey of wandering

□出来事 episode

□現代にも受け継がれている still practiced today

□神事の原点 core elements of religious ritua

□再現 re-enactment

古代人が怖れた「穢れ」

放浪の旅に出たスサノオは、途中で出会ったオオゲツヒメ（大気津比売神）を殺すという罪を犯してしまいます。この女神はスサノオに食べ物を求められたため、**密かに体内から食材を排出して提供**しました。あまりにも美味しいので、調理のようすをのぞき見すると、女神は口や鼻や尻から食べ物を出していたのです。**穢い物を食べさせた**と怒ったスサノオは、女神を殺してしまいます。そして女神の死体からは、**蚕や稲・麦などの穀物**が生まれ出ました。

スサノオが天上を追放されるときからオオゲツヒメを殺すまでの出来事には、古代人が抱いていた「おそれ」が端的に示されています。その一つは「穢れへの怖れ」です。罪を犯したスサノオは髪や爪を切られますが、これは身を清めるという意味の「禊ぎ」に通じる行為です。

死と再生への「畏れ」

そもそもスサノオは、黄泉国（死者の国）から逃げ帰ったイザナギが、穢れを清めようと川で「禊ぎ」をしたときに生まれた神です。これは、古代人が死者の**放つ異臭や腐乱する**ようすを「穢い」としていたことを物語っていますが、現代人にも通じる**嫌悪感**といってよいでしょう。

しかし、一方で古代人は、死は再生への始まりとしていたようです。スサノオが殺した女神の死体から穀物などが生まれ出たというのは、それを象徴するといえるでしょう。さらに、アマテラスが岩屋に閉じこもったのは死を意味し、再び姿を現したのは再生を意味しています。このように、古代人は「死と再生への畏れ」を神話という形で表現したとも考えられるのです。

The Ancients' Fear of Defilement

In his wanderings Susanoo met the goddess Ogetsuhime and murdered her. When Susanoo had asked her for something to eat, she had in secret produced the food from her own body. It was so delicious that Susanoo had taken a peep to see how it was prepared. He saw that she was producing the food from her mouth, her nose, and her rectum. Susanoo became angry that she had fed him something so filthy and killed her. From her body appeared silkworms, rice plants, wheat, and other grain.

Among the events that took place from the time Susanoo was banished from heaven until he murdered Ogetsuhime, there are many that show clearly the ancients' particular "fears." One of these is the fear of defilement. After committing the crime of murder, Susanoo cut his fingernails and hair. This was an act of purification.

Fear in the Face of Death and Resurrection

Susanoo was born when his father, Izanagi, escaped from the land of the dead, Yominokuni, and cleansed himself of defilement in a river. This episode tells of the ancient Japanese dislike of the smell of dead bodies and putrefying flesh. It is much the same in Japan today.

On the other hand, the ancients also thought of death as a new beginning. This is symbolized by the rice and other things that appeared from the dead body of the goddess Ogetsuhime. Furthermore, Amaterasu's hiding herself in a rock cave can be taken as signifying death and her reappearance as symbolizing resurrection. It can be said that the ancients signified their fear of death and rebirth in the form of this myth.

□密かに in secret
□食材を排出する drain away the food
□穢い物 something filthy
□蚕 silkworm
□穀物 grain
□端的に clearly
□〜に通じる行為 an act that links to/is associated with
□放つ emit
□腐乱する decompose
□嫌悪感 feelings of disgust

25

「出雲神話」の序幕

　やがてスサノオは、地上(葦原中国)に降り立ちます。その場所は出雲国の鳥髪(現在の島根県の船通山)で、肥の河(斐伊川)の上流にあたります。そこで川に箸が流れているのを見たスサノオは、人が暮らしていると考えてさらに上流へ向かい、一軒の家にたどり着きます。その家には老夫婦と若い娘がいて、皆で泣いていました。

　スサノオは家の中に入り、「お前たちは何者か？」と尋ねると、「私たちは国神オオヤマヅミの子孫で、アシナヅチとテナヅチという夫婦と娘のクシナダヒメです」との返事がかえってきました。さらに「なぜ泣いているのか？」と問うと、「私たち夫婦には八人の娘がおりましたが、ヤマタノオロチに毎年一人ずつ食べられてしまい、今年は最後に残ったこのクシナダヒメが食べられることになっています。それで、こうして泣いているのです」と。その説明によると、ヤマタノオロチは八つの頭と八つの尾、赤い目と常に血がしたたり落ちている腹を持つ巨大な蛇とのことでした。「では、わしに娘をくれないか。オロチを退治してやろう」というスサノオに対し、老父は「あなたは、どなたですか？」と尋ねます。「わしはアマテラスの弟で、天から降りてきたばかりだ」と答えると、老夫は畏まってスサノオの申し出を受け入れました。

★

　地上に降り立ったスサノオが八つの頭と尾をもつ大蛇を退治する話は、「出雲神話」の序幕にあたります。天上界の話とは異なり、地名が冒頭のように現代と比定できるのが特徴といえるでしょう。ヤマタノオロチとは、毎年、氾濫して人々を脅かす斐伊川やその支流、がけ崩れでむき出しになった山の赤い土のイメージを投影したものとも考えられています。

The "Izumo Myth's" Opening Scene

Eventually Susanoo descended to earth (the Central Land of Reed Plains) at Torikami in the land of Izumo (present-day Mount Sentsu, Shimane prefecture), which was on the upper reaches of the Hinokawa (now Hiikawa) river. Susanoo saw some chopsticks floating in the water, and thinking that people must be living on the river, he went further upstream until he arrived at a single house. There was an elderly couple living there and a young girl. They were all crying.

Susanoo went inside and asked, "Who would you be?" They answered, "We are Ashinazuchi and Tenazuchi, the descendants of the country god Oyamazumi, and this is our daughter Kushinadahime." When asked further, "Why are you crying?" they answered, "We had eight daughters, but each year one of them has been eaten by a serpent called Yamata no Orochi. This year the final daughter, Kushinadahime, is to be eaten. That's why we are crying." According to their explanation, the Yamata no Orochi possessed eight heads and eight tails, red eyes, and a belly from which blood was always dripping. When Susanoo said, "Give your daughter to me. I will vanquish the Orochi," the old man asked, "And who would you be?" Susanoo answered, "I am the younger brother of Amaterasu. I have just now descended from heaven." The elderly couple were properly impressed and agreed to Susanoo's proposal.

The story of Susanoo vanquishing the monstrous serpent with eight heads and eight tails is the opening scene of the "Izumo Myth." In contrast to the narratives of the heavenly realm, but similar to the beginning of this article, place names can be identified with those of modern locations, which can be said to be distinctive of the myth. The serpent might be seen as an analogy for the annual devastation of the Hiikawa river and its tributaries, when landsides revealed the red soil of the mountains.

□〜に降り立つ descend upon

□〜の上流 upper course of

□したたり落ちている dripping down

□退治する vanquish

□畏まる be in awe of

□序幕 opening act

□〜と比定できる can be identified as

□氾濫する overflow

□支流 tributary

□むき出しになった exposed

□投影したもの projection

ヤマタノオロチを退治する

26

　スサノオは、クシナダヒメを櫛に変身させ、みずからの髪に挿すと、アシナヅチに「強い酒を入れた器を八つ用意し、垣根を張りめぐらした八つの門の前に置いて待つように」と命じました。準備が整ってしばらくすると、八つの首をもつ大蛇ヤマタノオロチが現れ、それぞれの首を器に入れて酒を呑み出したのです。

　やがて、酔いが回った大蛇は寝てしまいました。それを見たスサノオは、剣を抜いて切りかかり、オロチを八つ裂きにして退治をしてしまったのです。そのときに流れ出た血で、肥の河は真っ赤に染まりました。

Slaying Yamata no Orochi

Susanoo transformed Kushinadahime into a hair ornament and inserted it into his hair. He then told Ashinazuchi to prepare eight containers filled with strong sake and to place one each before the eight gates in a surrounding fence. Not long after the preparations had been completed, the eight-headed Orochi appeared, put each of his eight heads into a container and began to drink.

Not before long, the sake took its effect, and the serpent fell asleep. Seeing this, Susanoo immediately drew his sword, cut Orochi into eighths, and killed him. The blood that flowed out from the serpent's body dyed Hinokawa red.

□櫛　hair ornament

□みずからの髪に挿す
inserted it into one's own
hair

□垣根　fence

□張りめぐらした　laid out in
a circle

□整う　be finished

□八つ裂きにする　tear into
eight pieces

出雲国にまつわる戦争の痕跡

27

　スサノオが切り裂いたヤマタノオロチの一本の尾から、すばらしい剣が出てきました。のちにアマテラスに献上され、天叢雲剣（草薙剣）と名づけられ「三種の神器」の一つとして天皇家に伝えられる霊剣とされます。オロチを退治した後、スサノオは出雲国須賀に宮殿を建て、クシナダヒメ（櫛名田比売、稲田姫命）と暮らしました。この場所は現在の須賀神社（島根県雲南市）と伝えられ、二人の間にはヤシマジヌミ（八島士奴美神）という神が生まれました。この神から六代目の子孫が、出雲の国づくり神話の主役であるオオクニヌシ（大国主神）です。

　ところで、神話はすべてが架空の物語ではなく、もとになった事実があるといわれます。オロチ退治の話に隠された事実についても、さまざまな仮説が存在します。例えば、切り裂かれたオロチから流れ出た血が川の水を真っ赤に染めたという表現は、大規模な戦争を暗示しています。その象徴が、剣です。出雲では豊富に産出する砂鉄の加工技術が発展し、なかでも鉄の武具は戦争を有利に進めるうえで効果的でした。また、スサノオという神名のスサとは出雲の地名の須佐に由来し、荒々しいという意味の「すさぶる」を想起させることから、実在した英雄がモデルになったという説もあります。

　いずれにしても、「出雲神話」は古代国家が形成される過程で生じた戦争の痕跡をとどめているといってよいでしょう。前述（32ページ）のように、この神話が戦いに負けて死んだ王（国神）の怨霊を鎮める目的で『古事記』に加えられたとするなら、この王とはスサノオにほかなりません。大和王権に滅ぼされた出雲の王の霊魂が祟りをおよぼさないように、オロチ退治をした英雄として祀りあげたとも読み解けるのです。

Traces of War in Izumo

After Susanoo had cut down Yamata no Orochi, a beautiful sword emerged from one of its tails. The sword was later presented to Amaterasu and given the name Ame no Murakumo no Tsurugi (Sword of the Gathering Clouds of Heaven) or the Kusanagi no Tsurugi (Grass-cutting Sword). It was one of the three regalia of the imperial house and passed down the generations as having miraculous powers. After Susanoo vanquished the serpent, he built a palace in Suga in Izumo and lived there with Kushinadahime. Suga is said to be where Suga shrine is now located in Unnan city, Shimane prefecture. Kushinadahime gave birth to the deity Yashimajinumi, whose sixth-generation descendant, Okuninushi, was the founder of the country of Izumo.

It is often said that myths are not all fiction, but that a kernel of truth lies at their core. About the vanquishing of Orochi, there are also many theories concerning the underlying facts. For instance, the description of the river flowing red with blood is said to intimate the carnage of full-scale war. This is symbolized by the sword. Izumo was rich in sand iron, which led to the development of the processing of iron, which itself was effective in the manufacturing of weapons of war. Furthermore, it is said that *Susa* in the name "Susanoo" comes from a place name in Izumo, and that it is associated with the word *"susaburu"* ("violent"). From this, it is theorized by some that Susanoo was modeled on an actual historical figure.

In any case, it seems fair to say that the "Izumo Myth" retains vestiges of a war fought in the process of establishing an ancient state. As discussed on page 33, if this myth was added to the *Kojiki* in order to placate the vengeful spirit of the king (Country God) who lost and died in the war, then this king must be none other than Susanoo. In order to prevent the spirit of the king of Izumo from placing a curse on the Yamato imperial line, Susanoo was revered as a hero who had vanquished the Orochi. The "Izumo Myth" can be interpreted in this way.

□霊剣 sacred sword
□架空の物語 fictional story
□仮説 hypothesis
□暗示する imply
□砂鉄 iron sand
□加工技術 processing technique
□荒々しい roughness
□すさぶる rustle
□いずれにしても In any case
□過程 process
□〜として祀りあげた be revered as something
□読み解ける can be interpreted as

28

[2] オオクニヌシ

三層から成る物語の舞台

『古事記』でスサノオが再び登場するのは、オオクニヌシ(大国主神)を主人公にした物語の中です。ここでスサノオは突如、根の堅州国(異界)の主神として現れます。スサノオが、どのようにして異界の主神になったかの説明がないのは、前に記したように大和王権に滅ぼされた出雲の王の霊魂を異界に封じこめようとしたためとも考えられるのです。

オオクニヌシには、オオナムチ(大穴牟遅神)、アシハラノシコオ(葦原色許男神)、ヤチホコ(八千矛神)、ウツシクニダマ(宇都志国玉神)など多くの別名があります。これは実際に存在した国々の神(国神)が一つになった、つまり統一されたことを想起させます。『古事記』では「出雲神話」に多くの紙数をさき、主人公のオオクニヌシを天上界の支配神アマテラスと同等の大神として扱っています。そしてオオクニヌシの物語は、地上界に降りてきたアマテラスの孫ニニギ(邇邇芸命)に「国譲り」をするところで終わるのです。

ところで、オオクニヌシの異名であるアシハラノシコオとは「葦原中国(地上)で最も魅力的な男」を意味し、スサノオが名付けたとされます。いうならばオオクニヌシを地上の支配者と認めたのが、異界の主神スサノオだったのです。実はオオクニヌシの物語の舞台は、天上界と地上界と異界の三層から成り立っています。それぞれの主神はアマテラス、オオクニヌシ、スサノオです。アマテラスとスサノオは姉弟、オオクニヌシはスサノオの七代後の子孫という関係ですが、これらが同時性をもって語られているのは神話ならではといえるでしょう。

[2] Okuninushi

The Stage of a Three-layered Play

Susanoo reappears in the *Kojiki* in a section of the tale in which Okuninushi is the protagonist. Here Susanoo suddenly appears as the main god of the underworld Ne no Katasunokuni. There is no explanation of how Susanoo became the ruler of this underworld, but it is possible that it was an attempt, as mentioned above, to confine the vengeful spirit of the defeated king of Izumo to the netherworld.

Okuninushi is also known by other names: Onamuchi, Ashiharanoshikoo, Yachihoko, and Utsukushikunidama. This calls to mind the fact that these different country gods (*kunitsukami*) actually became one—that is, that they were unified. In the *Kojiki* many pages are devoted to the "Izumo Myth," and the protagonist, Okuninushi, was treated on an equal footing with the grand ruler of heaven, Amaterasu. The story of Okuninushi ends when the grandson of Amaterasu, Ninigi, descends to earth, and rule of the country is handed over to him, an event known as *kuniyuzuri*.

Incidentally, Okuninushi's pseudonym Ashiharanoshikoo means the "Most Attractive Man in the Central Land of Reed Plains," which is said to have been given him by Susanoo. In other words, Susanoo, the ruler of the underworld, recognized Okuninushi as the ruler on earth. In fact, it can be said that the stage on which Okuninushi acted consisted of three layers: heaven, earth, and the underworld. The principal god of these three layers was Amaterasu, Okuninushi, and Susanoo, respectively. They were connected in that Amaterasu and Susanoo were siblings, and Okuninushi was the seventh-generation descendant of Susanoo. The fact that they could be spoken of as contemporaries is a special characteristic of mythology.

□ 突如 abruptly

□ 〜に多くの紙数をさく devote a significant amount of pages to

□ 同等の on an equal footing

□ 国譲り the act of ceding the country

□ 異名 pseudonym

□ 三層 three layers

□ 〜から成り立っている the act consisted of

□ 同時性 contemporaries

イナバの白兎

オオクニヌシ(大国主 神)の物語は、イナバ(因幡国、現在の鳥取県鳥取市)のヤガミ(八上)を舞台に始まります。この地の豪族の娘ヤガミヒメに求婚をするために、大勢の兄弟神が訪れました。その末弟がオオナムチ(大穴牟遅神、のちのオオクニヌシ)で、兄神たちに大きな荷物を背負わされていたので遅れて一人で歩いていました。

気多の岬にやってきたオオナムチは、海岸で泣き苦しむ兎に出会います。兎は毛がなく、丸裸でした。わけを尋ねると、兎はこう語りました。「私は隠岐島からきたのですが、海を渡るためにサメを騙して並ばせ、背を跳んでたどり着きました。ところが騙したことがばれて、怒ったサメに毛をむしり取られたのです」

「あなたの前に通りかかった神々は、泣いている私を見て、海水で体を洗い、風に当たると良いと勧めてくれました。そのとおりにすると、傷がなおるどころか皮膚が破れて痛みが増してしまいました。それで、こうして苦しんでいるのです」。それを聞いたオオナムチは兎を憐れみ、こうアドバイスをしたのです。「すぐに真水で体を洗い、蒲の花を敷いた所に寝転がりなさい」。早速、兎が実行すると皮膚の傷がなおり、白い毛がはえ、体は元どおりになりました。喜んだ白兎は、オオナムチに「ヤガミヒメは必ず、あなたの妻になります」と予言をしました。

The Hare of Inaba

The story of Okuninushi begins in Yagami in Inaba province (present-day Tottori city, Tottori prefecture). Many brother gods had assembled there to propose marriage to Yagamihime, the daughter of one of the powerful local clans. The youngest of the brothers, Onamuchi (later Okuninushi), had been made to carry some heavy luggage and was belatedly walking alone behind the others.

When Onamuchi came to Cape Keta, he happened upon a hare that was crying in pain on the beach. The hare had no fur; it was completely hairless. When asked the reason why, it said, "I came here from Oki island, and in order to cross the water, I tricked some sharks into lining up so that I could jump from the back of one to another and cross over. But when the sharks learned they had been tricked, they got angry and ripped off all my fur."

"When the gods who passed by here earlier saw me crying, they advised me to wash my body in seawater and dry it in the wind. But far from getting better, the skin broke and the pain got worse. That's why I am in such excruciating pain." Hearing this, Onamuchi felt pity for the hare and gave him this advice: "Immediately wash your body in fresh water and roll around on a bed of cattail flowers." Without losing a moment of time, the hare did just that, and his skin healed, his white fur grew back, and his body returned to normal. Overjoyed, the hare made a prediction about Onamuchi's future: "Without doubt, Yagamihime will become your wife."

□ 末弟 the youngest of the brothers

□ 岬 cape

□ 丸裸 naked

□ むしり取られた be ripped off

□ なおるどころか far from getting better

□ 憐れむ feel pity

□ 真水 fresh water

□ 蒲の花 cattail flower

□ 早速 Without delay

オオナムチが受けた試練

30

　一方、ヤガミヒメに求婚をした兄神たちは、ことごとく断られた**ばかりか**、「私はオオナムチと結婚をします」と言われてしまいます。その言葉に激怒した兄神たちは、殺害を計画します。オオナムチは2度にわたって殺されるのですが、そのたび天上の神に生き返らせてもらいました。そして、兄神たちがいる地上界から逃れるために向かったのは、異界である根の堅州国だったのです。

　根の堅州国でオオナムチはスセリヒメと出会い、結婚をします。実は、スセリヒメは異界の主神スサノオの娘でした。娘に結婚相手を紹介されたスサノオは、オオナムチに娘婿としてふさわしい男かどうか、3度にわたって**試練**を与えました。しかし、そのたびスセリヒメに助けられ、夫婦で異界から逃げ出すことに成功したのです。このとき、異界と地上界の**境界**まで追ってきたスサノオは、「お前は兄神たちを**征伐**して地上の王となり、オオクニヌシと名乗りなさい。そして、わが娘を**正妻**として迎え、大きな神殿を造ってそこで暮らすがよい」と叫びました。

Onamuchi Put to the Test

On the other hand, not only were all the older brothers' proposals rejected, but Onamuchi told them, "I will marry Onamuchi." Hearing this, the older brothers grew so angry that they began to plot to murder Onamuchi. Onamuchi was, in fact, killed twice, but each time the gods in heaven brought him back to life. And each time, in order to escape his brothers on earth, Onamuchi fled to the underworld Ne no Katasunokuni.

In Ne no Katasunokuni Onamuchi met Suserihime and married her. In fact, Suserihime was the daughter of the principal god of the underworld, Susanoo. Introduced to Onamuchi as a potential husband for his daughter, Susanoo tested him three times to see if he would be a fitting son-in-law. But each time Onamuchi was saved by Suserihime, and the couple successfully escaped the underworld. It was then that Susanoo, pursuing them to the border between the underworld and the earthly realm, shouted after them, "You will conquer your brother gods, become a king of the earthly realm, and be known as Okuninushi (Great Land Master). Then you will take my daughter as your lawfully wedded wife, build a magnificent mansion and live with her there."

□ ことごとく at every turn

□ 〜したばかりか not only that

□ 〜にわたって over, throughout, across

□ 試練 ordeal

□ 境界 border

□ 征伐する subjugate

□ 正妻 lawful wife

オオクニヌシの国造り

31

　地上界に戻ったオオナムチは、兄神たちを征伐して追い払い、オオクニヌシ（大国主神）と名乗って新しい国造りにとりかかります。これを助けたのが、スクナヒコナ（少名毘古那神）です。この神はカミムスヒ（神産巣日神）の子で、小さな葉の舟に乗って海のかなたからやってきました。体は**極小ながら**知恵者で、農耕や酒造の技術、薬草・温泉による治療法などをもたらしたとされます。

　カミムスヒは「造化三神」（48ページ）の一神で、地上界の創造神、穀物の神とされます。『古事記』ではオオクニヌシの物語にたびたび登場し、オオクニヌシの危機を救っています。さらにスクナヒコナに命じてオオクニヌシの国造りを助けさせたことから、出雲では国神の祖神と位置づけて崇拝されてきました。

　ところで、穀物神でもあるカミムスヒの子であるスクナヒコナが極小とされるのは穀物、とりわけ稲の種をイメージさせます。**しかもスクナヒコナは、海のかなたからやってきた外来神です。**このことからオオクニヌシの国造りは、海外から伝来したさまざまな技術によって大きく**進展した**とみることができます。国造りの成果を見届けると、スクナヒコナは姿を消します。海の彼方にあるとされる**不老不死の国**「常世の国」に帰ったと、『古事記』は記しています。

　稲作は、古代には新しい国造りの**基盤**でした。稲作によって定住化が促進し、人口が増え、**共同体意識**が高まったからです。共同体意識の核になったのが祖霊崇拝で、その集合体を「国魂」と呼びました。オオクニヌシの国造りとは、各地の国魂が集まって大きな国魂になったことを意味しているとも考えられます。

Okuninushi and Country Building

Returning to the earth, Onamuchi subjugated and vanquished his brother gods, assumed the name Okuninushi, and began the task of building a new country (*kunizukuri*). The god who assisted him in this work was Sukunahikona. Sukunahikona was the child of Kamimusuhi and had come from far across the sea riding a boat consisting of a small leaf. He was a tiny man of great wisdom and said to be the bearer of technical knowledge about agriculture and sake brewing as well as healing by medicinal herbs and hot springs.

Kamimusuhi, one of the Zoka Sanshin (Gods of Creation; see page 49), is said to be a creator god and god of grain on earth. He often appears in tales of Okuninushi in the *Kojiki* and saves Okuninushi from peril. Also, from the fact that he ordered Sukunahikona to help Okuninushi with country building, he has been worshipped as a country god.

Incidentally, Sukunahikona, who was the son of Kamimusuhi, the god of grain, was extraordinarily small, evoking the image of a seed or grain of rice. Moreover, Sukunahikona was a foreign god, having come to Japan from across the sea. From this we can see that Okuninushi's country building benefited hugely from various technical advances from abroad. After witnessing the successful completion of Okuninushi's country building, Sukunahikona disappears from the story. According to the *Kojiki*, he returned to the land of eternal life (Tokoyonokuni) across the sea.

Rice cultivation was the basis of building a new country. It not only encouraged the permanent settlement of people, but it also promoted increases in the population and a sense of local pride. At the core of this sense of local pride was ancestor worship of guardian spirits known as *kunitama* (spirits of the land). It is possible that Okuninushi's country building meant the collecting of individual *kunitama* from surrounding areas and making them into one large *kunitama*.

□極小 remarkably small
□ながら in spite of
□〜をイメージさせる evoke the image of
□しかも Moreover
□外来神 deity of foreign origin
□進展する progress
□見届ける witness
□不老不死 eternal life
□基盤 basis
□共同体意識 sense of local pride

32

アマテラスの大義

　オオクニヌシの国造りを、天上界で注視していたのがアマテラスです。「(地上の)葦原中国を、わが子に治めさせよう」と言い出しました。わが子とはアメノオシホミミ(天忍穂耳命)で、アマテラスの長男とされる神です。

　母神に地上の支配者になるよう命じられたアメノオシホミミが天の浮橋から地上をのぞくと、荒々しい国神がたくさんいたために怖気づき「地上は騒々しいので、行くのは無理です」と報告をしました。そこでアマテラスは神々を集め、善後策を協議しました。その中に、「造化三神」(48ページ)の一神であるタカミムスヒ(高御産巣日神)もいました。そして、タカミムスヒの娘はアメノオシホミミに嫁いでいることが明かされます。

　実は、「造化三神」は天地創成後に姿を隠していたのですが、オオクニヌシの物語でカミムスヒ(神産巣日神)とタカミムスヒが突然、登場します。しかも、カミムスヒはオオクニヌシが統一した地上界の祖神、タカミムスヒは天上界の最高神アマテラスの親戚という立場です。タカミムスヒはいわば天上界の創造神なのですが、これ以降は天神の地上界支配をサポートする人格神タカギノカミ(高木神)として度々現われるようになります。

　本来、天上界と地上界は、相互不可侵の共存関係にありました。しかし豊かになりつつあった地上界では、国神の間で戦乱が起きるようになったのです。最も強大なのは出雲国で、神名(大国主神)が示すようにオオクニヌシは地上界最高の国神とされていました。

　そのオオクニヌシを平伏させることで葦原中国を戦乱のない平和な国にしたい、というのがアマテラスの大義だったと考えられます。

Amaterasu's Greatest Wish

In the heavenly realm the deity paying particular attention to Okuninushi's country building was Amaterasu. She suddenly said, "I will make my son the ruler of the earthly Central Land of Reed Plains." This was Amenooshihomimi, her oldest son.

When Amenooshihomimi looked down upon the earth from the Floating Bridge of Heaven, he saw that there were many violent country gods and he shuddered in fear. He reported, "The earth is so chaotic that it is impossible for me to go there." Amaterasu then gathered the gods and discussed what could be done. Among these gods was Takamimusuhi, one of the Three Gods of Creation (see page 49). At this point we learn that Takamimusuhi's daughter is married to Amenooshihomimi.

After the creation of heaven and earth, the Three Gods of Creation vanish from the tale, but in the story of Okuninushi, Kamimusuhi and Takamimusuhi suddenly reappear. Moreover, Kamimusuhi is the guardian god of the country built by Okuninushi on earth, and Takamimusuhi is a relative of the principal god of the heavenly realm, Amaterasu. While Takamimusuhi is a god of creation, hereafter he often appears as the humanized heavenly god Takaginokami, who supports the rule of heavenly gods on earth.

In the beginning, the heavenly and earthly realms coexisted in a mutually inviolable state. However, as the earthly realm became richer, fighting broke out between the country gods. The strongest of them was Okuninushi (Grand Land Master), who was considered the paramount country god on the earth.

It was apparently Amaterasu's greatest wish that Okuninushi be brought to his knees and the Central Land of Reed Plains be made a peaceful land, a land without war.

□注視する pay close attention
□天の浮橋 Floating Bridge of Heaven
□怖気づく be intimidated
□騒々しい chaotic
□善後策 remedial measures
□協議する discuss
□〜に嫁いでいる be married to
□度々 often
□本来 originally
□相互不可侵 mutually inviolable
□共存関係にある coexist in a relationship
□戦乱 warfare
□平伏させる subjugate
□大義 greatest cause

33

天上界からの使者

　アマテラスは、地上界の支配者になったオオクニヌシに対して「国譲り」をするように説得する使者として次男のアメノホヒ（天穂日命）を派遣しました。しかしオオクニヌシを説得するどころか、逆に取りこまれて役に立ちませんでした。

　次に使者として選ばれたのがアメノワカヒコ（天若日子）ですが、この神はオオクニヌシの娘と恋仲になり結婚をしたのに報告しませんでした。アマテラスは雉の神に様子を見てくるように命じましたが、それを知ったアメノワカヒコは雉の神を矢で射殺してしまいます。そして雉の体を突き抜けた矢が天上界に届き、それをタカミムスヒ（高御産巣日神）が地上界へ投げ返すと、アメノワカヒコの胸に突き刺さって死んでしまいました。本来は不死のはずの天神が死んだことで、アマテラスは裏切られたのを知ったのです。

　三度目の使者として選ばれたのは、武勇にすぐれたタケミカヅチ（建御雷神）でした。地上界に降りたタケミカヅチは、出雲国の稲佐の小浜でオオクニヌシと対面し、「国譲り」を迫りました。オオクニヌシは、「そのことは、跡を継いだ息子たちがお答えするでしょう」と即答を避けました。そこでタケミカヅチは、息子のヤエコトシロヌシ（八重言代主神）を呼び寄せました。この神は、出雲国の祖神カミムスヒのお告げを聞いて「国譲り」を承諾すると、すぐに姿を隠してしまいました。

　さらにタケミカヅチが「他に伝えるべき人はいるでしょうか？」と尋ねると、オオクニヌシは「タケミナカタ（建御名方神）という息子がいます」と答えました。そのとき、大きな岩を手にしたタケミナカタが現れ、「力比べで決着をつけよう」と脅したのです。

A Messenger from the Heavenly Realm

Eventually Amaterasu sent her second son, Amenohohi, as a messenger to Okuninushi, who had become the ruler of the earthly realm, to persuade him to turn over rule of the earthly realm. Far from persuading him, however, it had quite the opposite effect.

The next deity to be chosen as a messenger was Amenowakahiko. He fell in love with the daughter of Okuninushi and married her, but didn't report this fact. Amaterasu ordered the Pheasant God to go and report on what he saw, but when Amenowakahiko learned of this, he shot the Pheasant God with an arrow and killed him. The arrow passed through the Pheasant God's body and reached the heavenly realm, where Takamimusuhi grabbed it and threw it back to the earth, piercing the chest of Amenowakahiko and killing him. Since a heavenly god, who were supposed to be immortal, had died, Amaterasu realized that she had been betrayed.

The third deity chosen to be a messenger was Takemikazuchi, who was known for his martial prowess. He confronted Okuninushi at Obama, Inasa, in Izumo and pressed him to transfer rule of the lands of the earthly gods to the heavenly deities (called *kuniyuzuri*). Okuninushi avoided a direct answer by saying, "My sons who succeed me will undoubtedly respond to this." Takemikazuchi then calls his son Yaekotoshironushi to him. Yaekotoshironushi, hearing the words of the guardian god of Izumo, agreed to the proposed *kuniyuzuri* and immediately concealed himself.

Takemikazuchi then asked, "Isn't there anyone else who should be informed?" Okuninushi answered, "There is my son Takeminakata." At that moment Takeminakata appeared with a large stone in his hand, saying threateningly, "Let's settle the matter by a test of strength."

□説得する persuade
□使者 messenger
□派遣する send
□取りこまれる be taken in
□雉 pheasant
□突き抜ける pierce through
□武勇にすぐれた renowned for martial prowess
□対面する confront
□迫る press
□跡を継ぐ succeed
□即答 immediate response
□承諾する consent
□決着をつける settle the matter

34

国譲り

　タケミカヅチは天上界最強の武人で、そもそもタケミナカタが勝てる相手ではありません。力比べに負けたタケミナカタは逃げ出しましたが、タケミカヅチはどこまでも追いかけ、ついに科野国（現在の長野県）の州羽の海（諏訪湖）で追い詰めました。「この地で謹慎するので、命だけは助けてください」と懇願するタケミナカタを許したタケミカヅチは、オオクニヌシと再び会って「国譲り」の確約を得たのでした。

　こうして地上界の葦原中国は、天上界の支配下に入ることになります。このとき、オオクニヌシは一つの条件を出しました。国を譲る代わりに、隠居をするための巨大な宮殿を建ててほしいというのです。そして、この要望が承認され、新たな統治者として天孫のニニギ（邇邇芸命）が天上界から降臨することになったのです（後述）。

　『古事記』や『日本書紀』では、この「国譲り」を最終的には話し合いで決定したというニュアンスで記述しています。しかし、実際は大和王権と出雲豪族との間で、長期にわたる熾烈な戦争がおこなわれた果てに、出雲豪族側が敗退したことが想起されます。出雲の豪族たちは、殺害されたり自殺に追いこまれたに違いありません。前述（40ページ）のように、古代人は「霊魂は永遠に続く」と考えていたため、怨念を抱いた死者の祟りを怖れました。怨霊を封じこめるという目的を付与されたのが巨大な宮殿、すなわち現存する出雲大社（島根県出雲市）と考えられるのです。にもかかわらず、「国譲り」神話でオオクニヌシは自らでは反抗することなく、あっさりと降伏しています。実は、オオクニヌシを主祭神とする出雲大社には、「国譲り」の真相をうかがわせる事象が存在しているのです。

"Transfer of the Land"

Takemikazuchi was the most powerful military figure in the heavenly realm, and not someone that Takeminakata could easily defeat. Having lost the test of strength, Takeminakata tried to run away, but Takemikazuchi was forever close behind, catching him in Shinano province (present-day Nagano prefecture) at the sea of Suha (Lake Suwa). "I will be on my best behavior while here on earth," begged Takeminakata. "Please spare me my life." Takemikazuchi forgave Takeminakata and met Okuninushi for a second time and received a firm commitment to transfer the rule of the earthly land to the heavenly realm.

This is how the earthly Central Land of Reed Plains came under the rule of the heavenly realm. At this point Okuninushi presented one condition. In return for relinquishing control of the Central Land of Reed Plains, he wanted a magnificent mansion built for his retirement. When this was done, the grandson of Amaterasu, Ninigi, descended to earth as its new ruler. We will take this up again in greater detail below.

The *Kojiki* and *Nihon Shoki* suggest that the matter was settled through peaceful discussion. But, in fact, we imagine that after many long and fierce struggles between the imperial line and the Izumo clan, the Izumo clan fell to defeat. Without doubt, its clansmen were either killed or driven to commit suicide. As mentioned on page 41, ancient Japanese believed that the soul or spirit was immortal, and they therefore feared the curses of the vengeful dead. A massive palace was built to confine the activities of these spirits, which exists today as Izumo Grand Shrine (Izumo Oyashiro; Izumo city, Shimane prefecture). Nevertheless, in the *kuniyuzuri* myth Okuninushi does not resist turning over the rule of the Central Land of Reed Plains, but acquiesces rather easily. In fact, the Izumo Grand Shrine, which is dedicated to Okuninushi, contains certain keys to the truth behind the relinquishing of Izumo.

□ 謹慎する be on one's best behavior
□ 懇願する beg
□ 確約を得る receive a firm commitment
□ 隠居をする retire
□ 降臨する descend
□ 熾烈な fierce
□ ～したことが想起される it is recalled
□ 祟り curse
□ 目的を付与された granted purpose
□ 主祭神 chief enshrined deity
□ 真相をうかがわせる事象 clues to the truth

巨大な神殿

35

　神話がすべて架空の話と言い切れないのは、ギリシャ神話に登場する都市トロイが19世紀末の発掘調査で実在が判明したことにも象徴されます。

　出雲大社は、古代から国内随一の高さを誇る神殿として知られていました。『古事記』に記されたオオクニヌシの表現によると、「高天原（天上界）に届くほど高くて、地底に届くほど深い柱をもった宮殿」という壮大なものです。現在の大社の本殿の高さは24ｍ。これだけでも充分高いのですが、西暦2000年に境内から巨大な柱が発掘され、前代には高さが48ｍもあったことが裏づけられました。これが意味するのは、「国譲り」のときにはすでに桁外れの巨大な神殿があり、その事実をオオクニヌシの言葉としてなぞったということにほかなりません。

A Gargantuan Shrine

That myths are not all fiction is shown by the excavation at the end of the 19th century of the city of Troy that appears in Greek mythology.

The Izumo Grand Shrine had been known since ancient times as the tallest building in Japan. According to Okuninushi's description in the *Kojiki*, "It was a magnificent structure whose pillars reached as high as heaven and as deep as the bottom of the earth." The present main hall is an impressive 24 meters high. However, in 2000 excavation in the shrine compound revealed that the previous height was 48 meters. This means that at the time of the *kuniyuzuri* there already existed a structure of extraordinary size, and Okuninushi's words were a manifestation of that fact.

□言い切れない difficult to say

□国内随一の the best in the country

□柱 pillar

□壮大な magnificent

□本殿 main hall

□境内 shrine compound

□裏づけられる confirming

□桁外れの extraordinary

□なぞった traced

出雲大社の謎

36

　出雲大社の主祭神は、オオクニヌシです。通常、本殿内の主祭神の神座は、参拝者の正面に位置しているのですが、オオクニヌシの神座はなぜか横向きで、しかも存在を隠すかのように板仕切りがあります。そして正面には「御客座五神」と呼ばれる神々の神座があって、参拝者はオオクニヌシでなく、これらの神々と相対していることになります。ちなみに、五神とは「造化三神」とそれに続いて現れた二神で、いずれも『記紀』の創成神話に登場する本源的な神々です(48ページ)。

　なぜ出雲大社では主祭神の神座を参拝者の正面でなく横向きに置いているのか。また、客神として創成神話に登場する五神を配しているのはなぜか。これらの謎こそが、「国譲り」の歴史的な事実を解明する手掛かりというべきでしょう。

　結論からいえば、出雲大社はオオクニヌシの隠居所、つまり文字通り隠れ住む場所ということです。この場合の「隠れる」とは、高貴な人の死を意味します。そして死者が怨念を抱いている場合は、死霊が祟りを及ぼさないように封印してしまうのです。

　『古事記』は、出雲には黄泉国(死者の国)と地上界の出入り口があり、イザナギ(伊邪那岐命)が悪霊が出てこないように巨石で封じたと記述しています。したがって出雲は死者の国に近い、つまり戦争によって多くの死者が出たことを暗示しているとも考えられます。出雲大社が本源的な五神を客神として招いているのは、オオクニヌシの怨念を畏れた人々の配慮と考えるのが順当でしょう。最古の神々の強い霊威によって封じこめなければならないほど、オオクニヌシの霊魂は脅威だったとみることができるのです。

The Mystery of Izumo Grand Shrine

Izumo Grand Shrine is dedicated to the god Okuninushi. Ordinarily the object of worship is located facing the parishioners, but for some reason here it is facing sideways with a wooden partition placed almost as if to hide its existence. Facing the parishioners are situated five "visiting gods" called *kyakujin*, and it is these deities that the parishioners are directly facing, not Okuninushi. Incidentally, the five gods are the Three Gods of Creation and two subsequent gods, all of which are fundamental gods that appear in the creation of heaven and earth in the *Kojiki* and *Nihon Shoki* (see page 49).

Why is the principal object of worship at Izumo Grand Shrine not facing the parishioners but rather located sideways to them? And why are the five *kyakujin* that appear in the creation myth placed where they are? The answers to these questions should provide some help in revealing the historical truth behind the *kuniyuzuri* of Izumo Grand Shrine.

To start with the conclusion, Izumo Grand Shrine was Okuninushi's place of retirement. In this case, when referring to people of noble birth, "retirement" meant "death." When the person who died bore a grudge against someone still alive, an attempt was made to confine the angry spirit and prevent it from placing a curse on the living.

The *Kojiki* says that there was a entry and exit between the land of the dead (Yominokuni) and the earthly realm, and that Izanagi blocked it with a huge rock to keep evil spirits from emerging from it. Therefore it can be thought that Izumo was near the land of the dead, that many people had died there in warfare. That Izumo invited to the shrine the five principal *kyakujin*, was, it seems fair to say, done out of consideration for those who feared Okuninushi's vengeful spirit. In fact, Okuninushi's immoral spirit was considered so menacing that it was necessary to call upon the mysterious power of the oldest and most powerful gods to restrain him.

□ 神座 the object of worship
□ 参拝者 worshipper
□ 板仕切り wooden partition
□ 相対する facing
□ 本源的な fundamental
□ 客神 guest deities
□ 配する be placed
□ 結論からいえば To start with the conclusion
□ 隠居所 place of retirement
□ 高貴な noble
□ 暗示する imply
□ 配慮 consideration
□ 順当である reasonable
□ 霊威 spiritual authority
□ 封じ込める restrain
□ 脅威である menacing

37

オオクニヌシの正体？

　『古事記』では天上界の最高神アマテラスと並ぶほどの大神とされたオオクニヌシとは、何者だったのか。そのヒントになるのが、数多いオオクニヌシの神名の一つの「国玉神」です。ちなみに、『古事記』では「宇都志国玉神」、『日本書紀』では「大国玉神」などと表記されています。

　「国玉（国魂）」とは、地上界の国神の魂を意味します。古代人は、これを地域共同体の核心としていたのです。大和王権の故地・纏向（奈良県桜井市）ではオオモノヌシ（大物主神）を国玉として、三輪山で祀っていました。実は、このオオモノヌシはオオクニヌシの分身ともされるのです。

　このようにオオクニヌシは、農耕を主とした日本各地の国神の大神として信仰を集めていたと考えられます。実際、現代でもオオクニヌシを祭神とする神社が各地に存在しています。神話では、オオクニヌシは6人の妻をもち、181人の子どもがいたとされますが、これはオオクニヌシを最高の国玉として信仰をしていた地域の広がりを示していると考えられます。

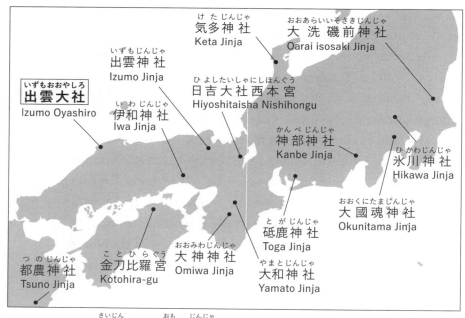

オオクニヌシを祭神とする主な神社
Principal Shrines Devoted to Worship of Okuninushi

Who Is the Real Okuninushi

In the *Kojiki* Okuninushi is seen as almost the equal of Amaterasu, the mightiest god of the heavenly realm. Who was this Okuninushi? A hint is provided by one of his many divine names—i.e., Kunitama no Kami (God of the Land Spirit). Incidentally, in the *Kojiki* he is referred to as Utsushi Kunitama no Kami, and in the *Nihon Shoki* as Okunitama no Kami, among other names.

"Kunitama" means the soul of a country god of the earthly realm. For ancient Japanese this god was the core of regional societies. The Yamato court's king had old ties with Makimuku (Sakurai city, Nara prefecture) and was known as the god Omononushi (Grand Entity Master); he was worshipped on nearby Mount Miwa. He is sometimes considered a double of Okuninushi.

In this way, it seems that Okuninushi, as the grand country god of farming in agriculture-oriented Japan, attracted innumerable adherents far and wide. Even today there are numerous shrines devoted to Okuninushi. According to mythology, Okuninushi had 6 wives and 181 children. This is an indication of the extent to which the belief in Okuninushi as a paramount king spread throughout the country.

□地域共同体 local communities

□故地 former land

□分身 double

□祭神 enshrined deity

38

[3] ニニギとホオリ

天孫降臨

　地上の葦原中国が支配下になったことで、天上界から**統治者**として派遣されたのがアマテラスの孫のニニギ（邇邇芸命）です。その父親はアマテラスが身に着けていた勾玉から生まれたとされる五神の一柱のアメノオシホミミ（天之忍穂耳命）で、皇太子という立場でした。しかも母親は創成神の一柱のタカミムスヒ（高御産巣日神）の娘で、いわば天上界の最高の**血筋**です。ニニギを天上界から送り出すにあたって、アマテラスは統治者の象徴となる「三種の神器」を与えたとされます(42ページ)。

　前述のように、古代の国造りの基盤となったのは稲作でした。『古事記』では、アマテラスが葦原中国を「豊葦原の千秋長五百秋の水穂国」と表現したことが記されています。豊かな葦原で長く久しく**稲穂**が実る国、という意味です。これが古代の**理想郷**だったというべきでしょう。そのような思いは、天上界の皇太子アメノオシホミミの漢字名の「忍穂」が大きな稲穂を意味し、その子の「邇邇芸」という神名が**賑々しく**（豊かに）稲穂が実るという意味を含んでいることからも**推測**できます。

　天神が地上界へ降りることを「**天降り**」といい、ニニギの場合は「天孫降臨」と**称**されます。このとき、ニニギはタカミムスヒの子で知恵者のオモイカネ（思兼神）や女神アメノウズメ（天宇受売命）などの五神を**引き連れ**ていました。いずれもアマテラスの「天の岩屋」の**引きこもり**事件(62ページ)で活躍した神々です。

[3] Ninigi and Hoori

Ninigi's Descent from Heaven

Now that the earthly Central Land of Reed Plains had been brought under its control, the heavenly realm sent Ninigi, the grandson of Amaterasu, to act as its ruler. Ninigi's father was Amenooshihomimi, born of one of the five gods from the curved jewels (*magatama*) worn on Amaterasu's person; his status was that of crown prince. Moreover, his mother was the daughter of the creator god Takamimusuhi; in other words, he came from the most noble lineage in the heavenly realm. When Amaterasu sent Ninigi down to earth, she presented him with the Three Imperial Regalia as symbols of his status as ruler (see page 43).

As mentioned above, the foundation for building a country (*kunizukuri*) was the cultivation of rice. According to the *Kojiki*, Amaterasu referred to the Central Land of Reed Plains as the Mizuhonokuni of Chiakinonagaihoaki in Toyoashihara. This simply means a country with lush reed fields and richly grown ears of rice, an ancient Japanese version of utopia. It was probably this notion that is contained in the two kanji characters of Amenooshihomimi's name that are read *oshiho*, meaning large ears of rice, and that his son's name, Ninigi (Thriving), suggests the growth of flourishing rice.

The descent of a heavenly god to earth is generally known as *amakudari*, but in Ninigi's case it is called *tenson korin* (the heavenly descent). On this occasion Ninigi took with him a total of five gods, including the wise son of Takamimusuhi (Omoikane) and the goddess Amenouzume. All of them played a role in the incident when Amaterasu hid in a rock cave (see page 63).

□ 統治者 ruler
□ 一柱 one of the gods
□ 血筋 lineage
□ 葦原 lush reed field
□ 久しく for a long time
□ 稲穂 ears of rice
□ 理想郷 utopia
□ 賑々しく lively
□ 推測できる we can guess
□ 天降り descent of a deity
□ 称される be called
□ 引き連れる take with
□ 引きこもり withdrawal

39

「日向神話」の始まり

　ニニギ一行が降り立った地は、日向の高千穂の峰とされます。ここが現在のどこかについては諸説(宮崎県の高千穂町、鹿児島県の霧島山、大分県の久住山など)ありますが、いずれにしても九州に比定されています。

　となると、天降り先が「国譲り」をしたオオクニヌシゆかりの出雲でないことに違和感を覚える人もいるはず。実は、オオクニヌシを主人公とした「出雲神話」の大半は『古事記』特有のもので、大和王権の正史である『日本書紀』では無視されているのです。

　つまり、『古事記』から「出雲神話」の記述を省くと、天孫が天降った地が日向ということに違和感がなくなります。それどころか、「日向」は太陽神アマテラス(天照大神)を強く意識した地名であり、また「高千穂」は豊かに稲穂が実るという意味を含むニニギという神名に呼応している、といった点で天降り先としての必然性を帯びています。

　では、なぜ「出雲神話」の多くを省いた『日本書紀』が大和王権の正史とされたのか？　おそらく、地方豪族を主人公にした神話は国の正史に組みこむほどの価値がないとしたためか、あるいは王権にとって不都合な事実が隠されていたためということなのでしょう。ちなみに後者には、「出雲神話」は王権に滅ぼされたオオクニヌシの鎮魂が目的だった、という説が有力です。

　「天孫降臨」の場面をきっかけに、神話は新たな展開をみせ始めます。それは、天神の子孫がどのようにして地上界を平定してきたのかを記述することを主眼にしたからです。その冒頭部分は「日向神話」ともいわれ、地上に降り立った天神が、大和王権(天皇と豪族)の先祖であることを強調しています。

The Beginnings of the "Hyuga Myth"

The place where Ninigi descended to earth was said to be a peak called Takachiho in Himuka. There are various theories as to its exact location (e.g., Takachiho-cho in Miyazaki prefecture, Mount Kirishima in Kagoshima prefecture, or Mount Kuju in Oita prefecture), but in either case it can be identified as somewhere in Kyushu.

If this is true, some readers may think it odd that the location of Ninigi's descent is not Izumo, founded by Okuninushi. The fact is that most of the "Izumo Myth", in which Okuninushi is the protagonist, is the particular property of the *Kojiki*, not the *Nihon Shoki*, which is the official history of the imperial family and which ignored the "Izumo Myth."

In other words, if the narration concerning the "Izumo Myth" is removed from the *Kojiki*, then the feeling of unease about Ninigi's descent to earth taking place in Himuka in Kyushu disappears. Quite to the contrary, "Himuka" (literally "facing the sun") is a place name with strong associations with the Sun Goddess, Amaterasu. Also, Takachiho (High Thousand Rice Ears) echoes the richness of rice implicit in the name Ninigi (Thriving), and at this point there appears an element of inevitability in the site of the descent from heaven.

Why, then, did the *Nihon Shoki*, without reference to the "Izumo Myth," become the official history of the Yamato imperial line? Most likely the reason is that, on the one hand, incorporating the myth of a local clan and its leader in the official history of the state was not seen as that important; or, on the other hand, there was some inconvenient truth hidden in the myth. In the latter case, incidentally, the most persuasive theory is that the "Izumo Myth" was an attempt to pacify the soul of Okuninushi, who had been overthrown by the imperial line.

★

With the descent of Ninigi to earth (*tenson korin*), Japanese mythology takes a new turn. Its principal concern is now the narration of how the descendants of the heavenly gods pacify the earthly realm. In the opening passages of what is known as the "Hyuga Myth," it is emphasized that the heavenly gods who descended to earth are the progenitors of the Yamato imperial line (the emperor and the imperial family).

□諸説 various theories

□ゆかりの relate to

□違和感を覚える think it odd

□特有のもの particular property

□それどころか Quite to the contrary

□呼応している echo

□必然性を帯びている inevitable

オオヤマヅミの呪い

　ニニギは、高千穂の近くの笠沙の岬で出会った美しいコノハナサクヤヒメ(木花佐久夜比売)に求婚をします。この女神は、山の神オオヤマヅミ(大山津見神)の娘でした。

　オオヤマヅミは、コノハナサクヤヒメとの結婚の条件として、姉のイワナガヒメ(石長比売)も一緒に嫁がせると要求したので、ニニギは仕方なく受け入れました。実は、この姉神は醜い容姿で、それを嫌ったニニギは**婚儀の翌日**に父神のもとに送り返してしまったのです。

　そこでオオヤマヅミは、「妹は美しい花のようだが、花はやがて散る。姉は醜いが、石のようにいつまでも変わらない。その姉を側に置かないというのは、天孫が自ら寿命を縮めてしまったということだ」と、**呪いの言葉を吐きました。**

★

　この**逸話**には、重要な意味が隠されています。それは、ニニギが**不死**とされる天神の子でありながら、呪いによって**死を免れない存在**になってしまったということです。

　東南アジアに広く伝えられている神話に、人間が神から贈られた石を拒んでバナナを食べてしまったので短命になったという話があります。こうした神話は**当然ながら海を渡って流入し、日本神話に影響を及ぼしている**と考えるべきでしょう。

　では、なぜこのような逸話を挿入しなければならなかったのか？ もし、ニニギが不死の存在のままなら、その子孫とされる天皇がなぜ死ぬのかが問題になるからです。

　ニニギを人間に近づけておくことで、そうした矛盾をあらかじめ解消しておこうとの意図があったと思われます。

The Curse of Oyamazumi

At Kasasa promontory near Takachiho, Ninigi met the beautiful goddess Konohanasakuyahime and proposed marriage. She was the daughter of the mountain god Oyamazumi.

As one of the conditions for agreeing to the proposal, Oyamazumi demanded that Ninigi also take in marriage the older daughter, Iwanagahime. There seemed no way around this, so Ninigi agreed. However, since he did not find the older daughter pleasing in appearance, the day after the marriage ceremony Ninigi sent her back to her father's home.

It was then that Oyamazumi placed a curse on Ninigi, saying, "The younger daughter is like a flower, but all flowers eventually wither. The older daughter is ugly, but like a rock she will always stay the same. By not placing the older at your side you have willingly shortened your own life."

Hidden in this story is an important point, which is this: while Ninigi is the child of a immortal god, by means of a curse he has become a mortal incapable of escaping death.

In a myth widespread throughout Southeast Asia, a man rejects a rock sent by a god and instead eats a banana, which shortens his life. It is not surprising that this tale should have made its way across the ocean, reached Japan, and influenced Japanese mythology.

This raises the question of why this story should be inserted into Japanese mythology. The reason is that if Ninigi should remain immortal, then the fact that his descendants—the imperial line—were mortal would become a problem.

Bringing Ninigi closer to ordinary human beings was apparently an attempt to forestall this problem ahead of time.

☐ 仕方なく There seemed no way around this,

☐ 婚儀 marriage ceremony

☐ 呪いの言葉を吐く place a curse

☐ 逸話 anecdote

☐ 不死である immortal

☐ 死を免れない存在になる become a mortal incapable of escaping death

☐ 拒む reject

☐ 当然ながら It is not surprising that

☐ 影響を及ぼす influence

☐ 挿入する insert

☐ 矛盾 contradiction

☐ 解消する resolve

41

火中の出産

　ニニギと婚儀をあげた翌日、コノハナサクヤヒメは**懐妊**をしてしまいます。それを知ったニニギは自分の子ではないと疑い、「父親は他の国神であろう」と妻に告げました。すると、コノハナサクヤヒメは「あなたの子なら無事に産まれ、他の国神の子なら無事ではすまないでしょう」と言い、戸口のない産室を造らせ、そこに**籠る**と火をつけました。そして**燃えさかる**産室の中で3人の男児を次々と産み、彼らがニニギの子であることを**証明**して見せたのです。

　子どもたちの名前は、**生まれた順に**ホデリ（火照命）、ホスセリ（火須勢理命）、ホオリ（火遠理命）といいます。いずれにも「火」の文字が入っているのが**特徴**です。出産の際に火を焚くのは東南アジアに広く見られる**風習**で、コノハナサクヤヒメの**火中の出産**は、古代日本にもそうした風習があったことを物語っています。

　『古事記』は、ニニギとコノハナサクヤヒメがその後どうなったかについては記していません。しかし、コノハナサクヤヒメは富士山の神霊として、現代に至っても各地の浅間神社に祭神として祀られています。富士山が優美な山容をもち、**加えて**活火山であることが、この女神のイメージと結びついたのでしょう。

　そして物語は、末弟のホオリを主人公にして展開されます。ホオリの**別名**は、山幸彦。一方、海幸彦という別名をもつのが長男ホデリです。ちなみに、「幸（幸い）」は「咲き」が語源という説もあり、母親のコノハナサクヤという名前にあやかったとも考えられます。また、山幸彦が兄たち**をさしおき**主役になったのは、山の神の子孫の正統性を強調したからにほかなりません。

Born in Fire

The day after the wedding ceremony Konohanasakuyahime becomes pregnant. Learning of this, Ninigi suspects that the child is not his and says to his wife, "The father must be another heavenly god." To this, Konohanasakuyahime replies, "If you are the father, the child will be safely born, but if you are not the father, then it will not," and she had a delivery room built without doors or windows and shut herself inside. The delivery room was set on fire, and from the blazing flames three baby boys were born one after another. Konohanasakuyahime had proven who was the father.

In the order of their birth, the names of the children were: Hoderi, Hosuseri, and Hoori. They are unusual in that they all include the word for "fire" in their names. Lighting a fire at the time of birth is custom widely practiced in Southeast Asia, and the story of Konohanasakuyahime giving birth in the midst of a blazing fire shows that Japan also possessed such a custom.

The *Kojiki* does not tell what became of Ninigi and Kono-hanasakuyahime after that. However, as the spirit of Mount Fuji, Konohanasakuyahime is worshiped as the dedicatory god of nearby Sengen shrine even to this day. It was undoubtedly Fuji's sublime form, in addition to the fact that it was still an active volcano, that associated Konohanasakuyahime with the mountain.

Thereafter the story continues to unfold with the youngest son, Hoori, as the leading figure. He is also known by the name Yamasachihiko (Bounty of the Mountains). The oldest son, Hoderi, is called Umisachihiko (Bounty of the Sea). Incidentally, one theory has it that *sachi* has its roots in the word for "bloom," and that it echoes the mother's name, which literally means "This flower blooms." Again, the reason Yamasachihiko became the protagonist, overlooking his elder brothers, was to emphasize the legitimacy of the mountain god's descendants.

□懐妊する become pregnant
□戸口 doorway
□産室 delivery room
□籠る shut oneself inside
□燃えさかる blazing flames
□証明する prove
□生まれた順に in order of birth
□風習 custom
□火中の the midst of a blazing fire
□山容 form of a mountain
□加えて in addition to
□別名 alternative name
□〜をさしおく put someone aside

42

兄弟の対立

　ホオリ(山幸彦)は山で獣を、ホデリ(海幸彦)は海で魚を獲って日々を過ごしていました。天孫ニニギの子どもたちが、このような暮らしをしていることには驚かされますが、ここにも神の子をより人間に近い存在にしておこうとの意図が感じ取れるのです。

　ある日、ホオリは兄のホデリに「たまには、お互いの持ち物を交換してみよう」と提案しました。そして、ホオリは兄の釣り道具を手に漁に出かけたのです。ところが、一匹の魚も釣れないどころか、兄が大事にしていた釣り針を失ってしまいました。ホオリは自分の剣を熔かして500個の釣り針を作って差し出しましたが、怒ったホデリは受け取ろうとしません。さらに1000個の釣り針を作っても、許してもらえません。

A Battle between Brothers

Hoori (Yamasachi) spent his days hunting in the mountains; Hoderi (Umisachi) spent his days fishing in the sea. It may seem surprising that the descendants of a heavenly god should be described as spending their time in this way, but this was apparently another attempt to make the gods more human-like.

One day Hoori made a proposal to Hoderi: "Once in a while why don't we switch our equipment?" So Hoori took his brother's fishing gear and went fishing. However, far from catching any fish, Hoori lost his brother's precious fishhook. Hoori melted down his sword and made 500 fishhooks from it, and gave them to Hoderi. But Hoderi was mad, and he refused to accept them. Hoori made 1,000 more hooks, but still Hoderi refused to forgive him.

□獲る catch
□意図 attempt
□感じ取れる can sense
□たまには once in a while
□釣り道具 fishing gear
□釣り針 fishhook
□熔かす fuse
□差し出す offer

海神の助け

　兄が許そうとしないので、ホオリは困り果てました。そこに現れたのが、シオツチ(塩椎神)です。この老神はホオリの悩みを聞くと、竹で編んだ小舟に乗せ、海神ワタツミ(綿津見神)の宮殿に行くように勧めました。

　海底の宮殿に着くと、ワタツミが出迎えてくれました。そして、その娘のトヨタマヒメ(豊玉比売命)と結婚することになったのです。楽しい日々が長らく続きましたが、ふと忘れていた目的を思い出したホオリ。ふさぎこんでいる夫の姿を不審に思った妻は、父神に相談をします。ホオリを呼んで理由を聞いたワタツミは、あまたの魚を集めて釣り針を探すように命じました。すると、のどに何かが刺さってものが食べられない魚がいるとの情報が寄せられたのです。

　こうして、兄の釣り針が発見されました。急いで地上に帰ろうとするホオリに、ワタツミは二個の大きな真珠を渡し、それを使って兄を降伏させる方法を教えました。地上に戻ると、ホデリが襲ってきました。しかし、水を自在に操ることができる二個の珠のおかげでホオリは危機を脱し、兄を従わせることができたのです。

　『古事記』では、兄弟の争いに敗れたホデリを阿多隼人という部族の祖としています。隼人とは現在の大隅半島(鹿児島県)周辺に勢力をもち海洋交易などをおこなっていた人々で、大和王権に対して反抗的だったようです。ホオリ(山幸彦)とホデリ(海幸彦)の争いは、そのような史的背景をうかがわせます。そして、ホオリが海神を味方につけて勝利したのは、ひとえに天孫ニニギの威光によるということを宣揚したものとも考えられます。

Saved by the God of the Sea

Since Hoderi refused to forgive him, Hoori was driven to distraction. Then Shiotsuchi appeared on the scene. When Shiotsuchi, an elderly god, heard Hoori's predicament, he wove a small boat out of bamboo and urged Hoori to take the boat and visit the palace of the sea god Watatsumi.

When Hoori reached the palace at the bottom of the sea, Watatsumi came out to greet him. By and by Hoori married Watatsumi's daughter Toyotamahime. They had many a happy day together, but eventually Hoori remembered the reason he had come there. Seeing how depressed her husband had become, Toyotamahime thought it odd and discussed the matter with her father. Once Watatsumi heard the truth from Hoori, he called together numerous fish and instructed them to hunt for the fishhook. That's when he received the report that one fish had something stuck in its throat and couldn't eat.

This is how Hoderi's fishhook was found. Just as Hoori was preparing to quickly return to earth, Watatsumi gave him two large pearls and told him how to use them to get Hoderi to forgive him. When Hoori arrived back on earth, Hoderi immediately attacked him. However, thanks to the two pearls, which could manipulate water to their hearts' content, Hoori evaded danger and forced Hoderi to do his bidding.

In the *Kojiki*, the defeated Hoderi is mentioned as the ancestor of the Atahayato tribe. The Atahayato wielded power in what is present-day Osumi peninsula (Kagoshima prefecture) and engaged in sea trade, among other things. They seem to have resisted the rule of the Yamato court. This historical background helps us understand the struggle between Hoori (Bounty of the Mountains) and Hoderi (Bounty of the Seas). The victory of Hoori, with the backing of the God of the Sea, was entirely due, it seems, to the influence of the heavenly Ninigi.

□困り果てる be driven to distraction

□竹で編んだ小舟 small boat woven from bamboo

□出迎える come out to greet

□長らく続く last for a long time

□ふと suddenly

□ふさぎこむ be depressed

□不審に思う think something odd

□あまたの numerous

□情報が寄せられる receive the report

□真珠 pearl

□降伏させる force to surrender

□水を自在に操る bend water to one's will

□珠 gem (pearl)

□危機を脱する evade danger

□従わせる subdue

□海洋交易 sea trade

□反抗的だ rebellious

□史的背景 historical background

□うかがわせる hint

□威光 authority

□宣揚したもの as a declaration

44

トヨタマヒメとの別れ

　ある日、海底の宮殿にのこしてきた妻が、ホオリがいる地上にやってきました。トヨタマヒメは**懐妊した**ことを告げ、地上で産みたいと言うのです。そして、浜辺に鵜の羽を使った**産屋**を建て始めましたが、でき上がる前に**産気づいて**しまいました。

　産室に向かうトヨタマヒメは「子どもを産むときは私の本来の姿になるので、けっして産室の中をのぞかないでください」と、ホオリに**念をおしました**。

　そう言われると逆にのぞいて見たくなるのが、**人の常**です。見たいという**誘惑に負けて**産室の中をのぞいた目に飛び込んできたのは、**苦しみのたうち回っている**サメの姿でした。怖ろしくなったホオリは、あわててその場を離れました。

　やがて出産を終えたトヨタマヒメは「あなたは私の本来の姿を見てしまいましたね。それは耐えられないほど、恥ずかしいことです。もう二度と、あなたの前には現れません」と言うと、海底に帰ってしまいました。そして、子どもの**養育係**として妹のタマヨリヒメ（珠依比売命）を地上につかわしたのです。

　産まれた男児は、ウガヤフキアエズ（鵜葺草葺不合命）と名付けられました。やがて成長すると養育係の叔母タマヨリヒメと結婚し、四人の子どもを得ます。

　天孫ニニギの降臨から始まった「日向神話」は、ここで**幕を閉じます**。同時に『古事記』の上巻（神代編）も終わり、**これ以降は天皇の事績と系譜を記した中・下巻になります。**

Parting with Toyotamahime

One day Toyotamahime, who had been left in the palace at the bottom of the sea, appeared on earth where Hoori was. She announced that she was pregnant and that she wanted to give birth on earth. She began building a delivery hut on a beach with cormorant feathers, but before she could finish she began to have labor pains.

As she made her way toward the delivery hut, Toyotamahime pointedly told Hoori: "At the moment of birth I will return to my true form, so whatever you do, please don't look into the delivery room."

But it seems a part of human nature to want to look at something when told not to look. Losing his fight with curiosity, Hoori peeked into the delivery room, and what should he see but a shark writing in pain. Overcome with fear, Hoori left the site as quickly as he could.

Finally finished giving birth, Toyotamahime said to Hoori, "You have seen me in my true form, something too shameful for words. I will never again appear before you." She returned to the palace at the bottom of the sea, leaving the upbringing of the child on earth to her younger sister Tamayorihime.

The child was named Ugayafukiaezu. When he grew up, he married his governess and aunt Tamayorihime, and they had four children.

The "Hyuga Myth," which began with the descent to earth of the heavenly god Ninigi, here draws to a close. This also marks the end of the first volume of the *Kojiki* ("The Age of the Gods"); the following second and third volumes deal with the achievements and genealogy of the Japanese emperors.

□ 懐妊する become pregnant

□ 鵜 cormorant

□ 産屋 delivery hut

□ 産気づく beging to have labor pains

□ 本来の姿 true form

□ 念をおす pointedly tell

□ 人の常 a part of human nature

□ 誘惑に負けて Losing his fight with curiosity

□ 苦しみのたうち回っている writhing in pain

□ 養育係 nurturing person

□ 幕を閉じる draw to a close

□ これ以降は after this

45

[4] イワレヒコ

大和を目指した大遠征

　地上界でのニニギ(邇邇芸命)の系譜は、ホオリ(火遠理命)、ウガヤフキアエズ(鵜葺草葺不合命)と続き、**四代目がイワレヒコ**(伊波礼毘古命)です。この名は磐余(現在の奈良県桜井市)という地名に由来し、橿原宮で即位したと『古事記』には記されています。このことから、イワレヒコを初代天皇(神武天皇)とするのです。

　イワレヒコは日向の高千穂宮を拠点としていましたが、都を置くのにふさわしい土地を求めて東に向かおうと決めました。そして、美々津(現在の宮崎県日向市)の浜から兵を乗せた**船団**を組み**船出**をしたのです。船団は九州の北部を経て、瀬戸内海を通って熊野(和歌山県)に至り、そこで上陸して大和を目指しました。その間、竺紫(福岡県)に1年、阿岐(広島県)に7年、吉備(岡山県)に8年**滞在**したとされます。

　この**大遠征**を、「神武東征」といいます。

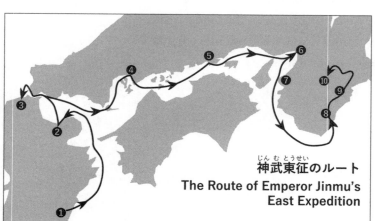

神武東征のルート
The Route of Emperor Jinmu's
East Expedition

❶	美々津	Mimitsu
❷	宇沙	Usa
❸	岡田宮	Okadanomiya
❹	多祁里宮	Takerinomiya
❺	高島宮	Takashimanomiya
❻	白肩津	Shirakatanotsu
❼	男之水門	Onominato
❽	熊野	Kumano
❾	吉野	Yoshino
❿	橿原	Kashihara

[4] Iwarehiko

The Great Excursion to Yamato

Ninigi's genealogy on earth consists of Hoori, then Ugayafuki-aezu, and fourth-generation Iwarehiko. The name "Iware" is derived from a place which is now in Sakurai city, Nara prefecture. This is where, according to the *Kojiki*, Iwarehiko was enthroned at the Kashihara palace. Iwarehiko thus became the first Japanese emperor or sovereign (*sumeramikoto*), Emperor Jinmu.

Iwarehiko had the Takachiho palace in Himuka as his base, but then decided to find a more suitable place for his capital further to the east. From the beach at Mimitsu (present-day Hyuga city, Miyazaki prefecture) he set sail with a convoy of soldiers. Via northern Kyushu he passed through the Seto Inland Sea and arrived at Kumano (Wakayama prefecture). There he landed and headed for Yamato. During this time, he stayed one year at Tsukushi (Fukuoka prefecture), seven years at Aki (Hiroshima prefecture), and eight years at Kibi (Okayama prefecture).

This monumental expedition is called the East Expedition of Emperor Jinmu.

□四代目 fourth generation
□〜にふさわしい suitable for
□船団 fleet
□船出する set sail
□目指す head for
□滞在する stay
□遠征 expedition

熊野上陸

46

　イワレヒコが、熊野から大和へ向かったのには理由がありました。当初は白肩津（現在の東大阪市）から生駒山を越えて大和へ入ろうとしたのですが、ナガスネヒコ（那賀須泥毘古）の軍に襲われて兄のイツセ（五瀬命）が**矢傷**を受けてしまいます。このことで、イワレヒコは「太陽（東）に向かって軍を進めようとしたので、天が怒ったに違いない」と思い、紀伊半島を回って熊野から上陸することにしたのです。その船旅の途中、イツセは矢傷がもとで死んでしまいました。

　熊野ではタカクラジ（高倉下）という男が、**一振りの剣**を持ってイワレヒコの前に現れました。男は「この剣は、私の夢の中で天の神々があなたに渡すようにと告げられ、**地上に降された**ものです。剣の霊力で地上を平定するようにと、天の神々は願っておられます。そして道案内をするヤタガラス（八咫烏）を、天**から差し向けよう**とおっしゃっておられました」と言ったのです。

　天上界からの**加護**を得て**勢いをつけた**イワレヒコと兵たちは、**険しい山中を**進んで宇陀に至り、そこでウカシ（宇迦斯）兄弟と戦って**勝利**しました。その後、ヤソタケル（八十建）、シキ（師木）兄弟、トミヒコ（登美毘古）などを次々と**打ち破って**、大和を平定したのです。

　イワレヒコの東征が、**最終的に**高天原の神々、特にアマテラス（天照大神）とタカギノカミ（高木神）の**支援**によって**目的を達成した**という点に、大和朝廷のアイデンティティが**示されて**います。

Landing at Kumano

There was a reason for Iwarehiko's setting off for Yamato from Kumano. At first he had planned to head for Yamato from Shirakatanotsu (present-day Higashiosaka city) by crossing Mount Ikoma. But he was attacked by Nagasune, and his older brother, Itsuse, was wounded by an arrow. This made Iwarehiko think: "Since I was advancing my army toward the sun [the east], this must have angered the heavens." He decided to go around the Kii peninsula and land at Kumano. In the midst of this journey, Itsuse died from the wound caused by the arrow.

In Kumano a man called Takakuraji appeared before Iwarehiko bearing a sword. He said, "This sword was given to me by the heavenly gods in a dream, saying it should be handed over to you. They hope its mysterious power will be used to bring peace to the earth. They will also send a eight-span crow to guide you on your way."

Having gained the protection of heaven, Iwarehiko and his soldiers grew ever more bold. Pushing their way through the mountains, they reached Uda and defeated the Ukashi brothers. Thereafter they subjugated Yasotakeru, the Shiki brothers, Tomihiko, and others, bringing peace to Yamato.

In the end, it is in the success of Jinmu's east expedition, with the support of the heavenly gods, especially Amaterasu and Takaginokami, that the identity of the Yamato court is established.

☐矢傷 arrow wound

☐〜がもとで死ぬ die from

☐一振りの剣 a single sword

☐地上に降された be brought down to earth

☐霊力 spiritual power

☐八咫烏 Yatagarasu: a three-legged crow in Japanese mythology and a deity of guidance

☐〜から差し向ける be sent from

☐加護 protection

☐勢いをつけた be energized

☐険しい steep

☐打ち破る defeat

☐最終的に in the end

☐支援 support

☐目的を達成する achieve the goal

もう一人のイワレヒコ？

　イワレヒコは、大和（現在の奈良県）の橿原に建てた宮殿で天皇に即位したと『古事記』は記しています。しかし、前述（38ページ）のように、実在の人物かどうかは不明です。また、大和朝廷の発祥地が纏向（現在の奈良県桜井市）であるとの説が有力であることから、橿原宮での即位は**現実的ではない**とも指摘されています。

　実は、イワレヒコという名前がふさわしい天皇がもう一人いるのです。26代の継体天皇で、実在したことがはっきりしています。この天皇の王宮は、磐余の玉穂という所にありました。さらに、九州**との関わりが深い**という点で、「神武東征」の神話は継体天皇の時代に創られたものではないかともいわれるのです。その在世の西暦527年、北九州で大規模な反乱が起きました。有力豪族の筑紫磐井（石井）の乱です。大和朝廷は軍を派遣し、1年半もの戦いの後、ようやく平定しました。このとき、九州南部の日向の豪族たちは大和朝廷側についていたのです。「神武東征」が日向を**起点**に始まり、北九州から瀬戸内海を経て熊野に至り、そこから大和に入ったとするルートは、逆に見れば大和朝廷が筑紫磐井の**討伐**に向かったルートということになるでしょう。

　『記紀』が大和朝廷の正当性を神話によって記述しているのは、天皇が天上界の最高神アマテラス（天照大神）の子孫であるとの**権威づけ**のみならず、朝廷を支える豪族たちも天神の子孫であり、**野卑な国神とは格が違う**ことを示したものと考えられます。例えば、朝廷の**祭祀**を担当した中臣氏（後の藤原氏）の祖神は、「天孫降臨」の際にニニギ（邇邇芸命）に**随行した**アメノコヤネ（天児屋命）とされました。

Another Iwarehiko?

According to the *Kojiki*, Iwarehiko built a palace at Kashihara in Yamato (present-day Nara prefecture) and assumed the throne as sovereign of the country (*sumeramikoto*). However, as mentioned on page 39, it is uncertain whether Iwarehiko was, in fact, a historical person. Moreover, since the theory that the origins of the Yamato court are to be found in Makimuku (present-day Sakurai city, Nara prefecture) is very strong, it has been pointed out that the enthronement at Kashihara is unrealistic.

As it happens, there is another emperor for whom the name Iwarehiko is appropriate. This is the 26th emperor Keitai, whose existence is without doubt. His royal palace was in a place called Tamaho in Iware. In addition, given the deep connections with Kyushu, it is said that the story of the East Expedition of the Emperor Jinmu must have been created during the reign of Emperor Keitai. During his lifetime, in 527, a large-scale revolt occurred in Kyushu. It is known as the Tsukushi no Iwai revolt. After more than a year and a half of fighting, the Yamato court's army finally pacified the country. It was then that the powerful local clans of Himuka in southern Kyushu sided with the Yamato court. The route followed on Jinmu's east expedition, starting in Himuka, proceeding from northern Kyushu to the Inland Sea to Kumano, and finally reaching Yamato, must have been the route followed by the Yamato army in crushing the Tsukushi no Iwai revolt.

The *Kojiki* and *Nihon Shoki* attempted to legitimize the authenticity of the Yamato court through mythology by establishing that the emperor was the descendant of Amaterasu, the supreme god in the heavenly realm. But it further showed that the powerful families that supported the court were also descendants of heavenly gods (*amatsukami*) and of a different rank from mere earthly country gods (*kunitsukami*). For example, the guarding god of the Nakatomi clan (later called the Fujiwara clan), which was in charge of rites and ceremonies, was Amenokoyane, who accompanied Ninigi when he descended to earth.

□ 発祥地 birthplace
□ 現実的ではない unrealistic
□ 〜との関わりが深い deep connections with
□ 在世 lifetime
□ 反乱 revolt
□ 起点 starting point
□ 討伐 subjugation
□ 権威づけ establish the authenticity
□ 野卑な vulgar
□ 〜とは格が違う in a different league
□ 祭祀 religious rituals
□ 随行する accompany

48

高まる天皇の権威

『記紀』が示す天皇は、神武に続く2代の綏靖から9代の開化までの8人についての記述は少なく、そのことから「欠史八代」とも呼ばれます。そして、10代の崇神以降は再び事績の具体的な記述が多くなり、朝廷が権勢を増していったことがうかがえるのです。もちろん、それらは『記紀』がまとめられた8世紀初頭においても、はるか大昔の話でフィクションにほかなりません。

しかし、そこには、創作だからとして看過できない"何か"が隠されていると思われるのです。例えば、15代の応神の治世には朝鮮半島との交流が盛んになり、高度な稲作技術や鉄の農具が輸入されて農地開発が進みました。一方、武力による衝突も増えてきました。応神の母の神功皇后は、みずから朝鮮半島に兵を連れて出向き新羅を平定したとされますが、この武勇伝は大和朝廷の経済・軍事力が大きくなった表れと見ることができるでしょう。

天皇の権威の高まりとともに、その座をめぐって争いが起きるのが人の世の常です。応神が亡くなったときも、王子の間で跡目争いが起きました。兄が末弟に水死させられ、末弟も早くに亡くなったため、のこった一人が天皇の座につきました。それが16代の仁徳で、貧しい人民のために3年間にわたって税をとるのを止めるなど仁政をおこないました。その仁徳の悩みは、嫉妬深い皇后が朝廷の女性たちに意地悪をすることでした……。

このように『記紀』は天皇の系譜や事績だけでなく、それにまつわる人間模様もさりげなく記しています。この傾向は、当然ながら正史である『日本書紀』よりも『古事記』に強く表れているのです。その意味で、天皇の子であるヤマトタケル（倭建命）の悲劇を描いた物語（116ページ〜）は、私たちの胸に迫るものがあります。

The Rise in the Emperor's Prestige

Of the emperors (*sumeramikoto*) mentioned in the *Kojiki* and *Nihon Shoki* after Jinmu, very little is said about the 2nd emperor Suizei to the 9th emperor Kaika. This is sometimes referred to as the "period of the eight undocumented monarchs." From the 10th emperor (Sujin) onward, the accounts of specific achievements once again becomes more detailed. The power and influence of the court had evidently become stronger. However, these accounts were compiled by the *Kojiki* and *Nihon Shoki* at the beginning of the 8th century, and even then they were nothing but fiction dealing with the distant past.

However, just because a myth is fiction does not mean that there is nothing of importance hidden within it. For example, during the reign of the 15th emperor, Ojin, exchange with Korea was vigorous, and with the importing of rice technology and iron tools, the development of agricultural land grew apace. At the same time, armed conflict also increased. Ojin's mother, Empress Jingu, is said to have led an army to the Korean peninsula and subjugated the kingdom of Silla; this tale can probably be seen as an indication of the growing military and economic strength of the Yamato court.

With the growth of the emperor's power and prestige, it is perhaps only natural that conflict should arise over who should next occupy the throne. When Emperor Ojin died, a conflict ensued between the royal princes over which should succeed Ojin. The oldest brother was drowned by the youngest, and the youngest himself died at an early age, leaving a remaining brother to ascend the throne. This was the 16th emperor, Nintoku. He carried out humane policies and ceased taxing the poor for three years. Nintoku's chief worry was the spitefulness with which the jealous empress treated the court ladies.

Thus the *Kojiki* and *Nihon Shoki* not only record the genealogy and achievements of the emperors, but they also indirectly depict the fabric of human relations. Of course, this tendency appears more strongly in the *Kojiki* than the *Nihon Shoki*, given the latter's position as official history. In that sense, the tragic story of Yamato Takeru, the son of the emperor (see page 117 and thereafter), is all the more moving.

- □ 欠史八代 The Eight Emperors of Unknown Lineage
- □ ～以降は From ～ onwards
- □ 権勢 power and authority
- □ うかがえる suggesting
- □ 看過できない cannot be ignored
- □ 皇后 Empress
- □ みずから on one's own initiative
- □ 武勇伝 tales of valor
- □ 座 throne
- □ 跡目争い power struggle for succession
- □ 仁政 benevolent rule
- □ 嫉妬深い envious
- □ 意地悪 spitefulness
- □ 人間模様 the tapestry of human interactions
- □ さりげなく subtly
- □ 悲劇 tragic tale

49

[5] ヤマトタケル

悲劇の旅路

　12代景行天皇の子どもの中に、オウス（小碓命）という王子がいました。この王子は乱暴者で、宮廷で怖れられる存在でした。あるとき、兄のオオウス（大碓命）が食事にこなかったのを怒った天皇が「戒めてきなさい」とオウスに命じました。その言葉を「処刑しなさい」と受けとったオウスは、兄を**惨殺**してしまったのです。

　それを知った景行天皇は、オウスの**残虐性**を恐れ、宮廷から追放しようとしました。その**口実**にしたのが、ヤマト朝廷に従わない地方豪族の討伐でした。最初に向かわされたのは、はるか遠くの九州南部です。そこではクマソタケル（熊襲建）兄弟が、反乱を起こしていました。長旅を経て現地にたどり着いたオウスは、クマソ軍の勢いが強いことを知り、**一計を案じます**。女装して宴会の席に忍び込み、隠し持った短刀で兄弟を殺そうというのです。計画は成功して兄は**即死**、弟は死の直前にオウスの**素性**を知ると「あなたは今後、ヤマトタケルと名乗りなさい」と言って**息絶えました**。

　クマソを平定し、ヤマトタケルと名を変えたオウスは、出雲でイズモタケル（出雲建）を討伐して**凱旋**しました。しかし、景行天皇は**間髪を入れず**、今度は東国への遠征を命じたのです。ここに至って、ヤマトタケルは父に嫌われていることを**察知**しました。そこで東国へ向かう途中で、叔母のヤマトヒメ（倭比売命）がいる伊勢を訪ね、「天皇は私が死ぬことを望んでおられるようです」と**嘆**きました。

　わが子の死を望む親と、その親のために**死を賭して戦い続け**ねばならない子。ヤマトタケルの悲劇の**構図**です。

[5] Yamato Takeru

Fateful Journeys

Among the children of the 12th emperor, Keiko, was prince Ousu. He was rough and unruly and feared at the court. One day his older brother, Ohusu, did not appear for dinner, and the angered emperor told Ousu to reprimand him. Ousu took these words to mean that he should kill Ohusu, which he brutally did.

Learning of this, and fearing Ousu's brutality, Keiko tried to banish him from the court. The reason he gave was the need to suppress rebellious clans in the provinces. Ousu was initially sent to far-off southern Kyushu, where the Kumasotakeru brothers were in rebellion. After a long, arduous journey, Ousu arrived at his destination. Finding that the Kumaso warriors were stronger than expected, he came up with a plan, which was to dress as a woman, sneak into a party being held, and kill the two brothers with a concealed dagger. The plan was a success. The older bother died immediately, and the younger, learning of Ousu's identity as he breathed his last, said, "From this day on, you must go by the name of Yamato Takeru [Yamato the Brave]."

Having pacified the Kumaso and changed his name to Yamato Takeru, Takeru subjugated the Izumotakeru in Izumo and returned home in triumph. However, without losing a moment, Emperor Keiko immediately ordered him on a expedition to the East. By now Takeru realized that he was not in the emperor's good favor. On his way to the East he stopped by Ise and lamented to is aunt Yamatohime, "The emperor wants to see me die."

The father who wished for the death of his son. The son who continued to fight for the sake of his father, risking all. This was the life of Yamato Takeru.

□ 戒める warn
□ 処刑する put to death
□ 惨殺する massacre
□ 残虐性 ruthlessness
□ 口実 excuse
□ 一計を案じる devise a plan
□ 宴会 banquet
□ 忍びこむ infiltrate
□ 即死 instant death
□ 素性 background
□ 息絶える take one's last breath
□ 凱旋する return victorious
□ 間髪を入れず without hesitation
□ 察知する sense
□ 嘆く mourn
□ 死を賭して戦く fight for one's life
□ 構図 arrangement

たび重なる災難

　ヤマトヒメは、別れを告げるヤマトタケルに**神剣**と**守り袋**を授けました。神剣はニニギ（邇邇芸命）が「天孫降臨」のときにアマテラス（天照大神）に**託された**ものです。この神剣と守り袋は、ある豪族との戦いで役に立ちました。ヤマトタケル軍は広い野原に**誘い込まれ**、**火攻め**にあったのです。そのとき神剣で草を**なぎ払い**、守り袋の中にあった**火打ち石**で**向火**をたいて危うく難を逃れました。その場所は焼津（現在の静岡県静岡市）と呼ばれ、神剣は草薙剣と命名されました。

　ヤマトタケルは更に東へと進軍します。走り水の海（現在の浦賀水道）を船で渡ろうとすると、**荒ぶる海峡の神**が行く手をはばみました。荒れ狂う海に身を投じて神の怒りを鎮めたのが、妻のオトタチバナ（弟橘比売命）でした。悲しみが癒えぬまま、ヤマトタケルは進軍を続けたのです。

Recurrent Catastrophe

As Takeru said his farewells, Yamatohime presented him with a divine sword and a pouch containing a lucky charm. The sword was the one that Amaterasu had given Ninigi when he descended to earth. The sword and the pouch had proven useful in the fighting with a certain powerful clan. Takeru's forces had been lured onto a broad plain and surrounded by fire. He had employed the sword to cut down the grass and a flint in the pouch to start a backfire, managing to escape by the skin of his teeth. The place where this happened is called Yaizu (present-day Shizuoka city, Shizuoka prefecture). The sword was give the name Kusanagi no Tsurugi (Grass-cutting Sword).

Takeru and his troops pressed on further east. He attempted to cross Hashirimizu no Umi (present-day Uraga Channel) by boat but was thwarted by the malevolent channel god. In order to pacify the god, Takeru's wife, Ototachibana, threw herself into the roiling waters and drowned. With his heart still unhealed, Takeru continued his march.

□神剣 divine sword

□守り袋 a pouch containing a lucky charm

□授ける present

□託された be entrusted

□誘い込む lure

□火攻めにあう be attacked by fire

□草をなぎ払う knock away the weeds

□火打ち石 flint

□向火をたく light a backfire

□危うく難を逃れる narrowly escape danger

□水道 waterway

□荒ぶる raging

□海峡 strait

□行く手をはばむ obstruct one's way

□身を投じる throw oneself

□鎮める pacify

□癒えぬ unhealed

51

白鳥になった魂

　ヤマトタケルは東国を巡って敵対する豪族たちを倒し、帰路につきます。その途中で再会したミヤズヒメ（見夜受比売命）と結婚をし、近江(現在の滋賀県)の伊吹山の悪神を退治に出向きました。しかし、山の神の祟りで大傷を受け、大和を目前にして力尽きました。その魂は、白鳥となって大空の彼方に飛んでいったということです。

　幾度も難を乗り越え、あまたの敵を打ち負かした英雄がなぜ死ぬことになったのか？　それは、神剣を新妻のもとに置いたまま出掛けたからとされています。つまり、ヤマトタケルは天神の加護のない人間として死を迎えたということです。しかし、この物語の作者は、その魂が白鳥になって飛んでいったというところに救いを与えています。

★

　実は、ヤマトタケルの物語の結末は『古事記』と『日本書紀』では異なっているのです。『古事記』は白鳥となったヤマトタケルの魂は父のいる大和を素通りして飛んで行きますが、『日本書紀』ではいったん大和に留まります。ここに、両書が書き表された目的の違いが端的に示されているのです。『古事記』はヤマトタケルが父との確執を抱いたまま死んだとし、『日本書紀』は天皇のために身を捧げた英雄として描いています。『日本書紀』が親子の確執にまったく触れていないのは、正史として天皇の正当性を記述することを第一義としたことで人間的要素をできるだけ排除する必要があったためと思われます。

　また、ヤマトタケルは九州から東北までの各地を転戦していますが、これは大和朝廷が派遣した軍の指揮官たちを集約して一人の英雄物語に仕立てたと考えるのが自然でしょう。

His Soul Becomes a White Bird

Takeru made the rounds of the eastern countries, defeated opposing local lords, and set off for home. On the way he happened to meet Miyazuhime and married her, and then made his way to annihilate the malevolent god of Mount Ibuki in Omi (present-day Shiga prefecture). However, he received a serious injury from a curse placed on him by the mountain god and breathed his last just before reaching Yamato. His soul is said to have turned into a white bird which flew off into the distant sky.

Why did this hero, who had met and defeated numerous foes, come to met his end? The reason is said to be that he had left the divine sword with his new wife when he departed for his last expedition. That is, Takeru met his end as a human being, without the protection of the heavenly gods. The only consolation that the writer of this tale provided Takeru was that his soul turned into a white bird flying high in the sky.

However, the fact of the matter is that the *Kojiki* and *Nihon Shoki* give two different endings to Takeru's tale. In the *Kojiki* the white bird embodying Takeru's soul flies past Yamato where his father is, without stopping, but in the *Nihon Shoki* the white bird makes a short stop in Yamato. Here we can clearly see the different purposes for which the two books were written. In the *Kojiki* Takeru dies still bearing ill feelings toward his father, but in the *Nihon Shoki* he is depicted as a hero who gave his all for the emperor. The reason the *Nihon Shoki* does not take up the feud between father and son is that, being an official history, its primary purpose was to legitimize the status of the emperor, for which goal the depiction of particular human characteristics would best be avoided.

Another way of viewing Takeru is as a representation of all the leaders of the imperial forces who fought in distant Kyushu in the south to far-off Tohoku in the north.

□〜を巡る travel through

□敵対する hostile

□出向く make one's way

□目前にして just before reaching

□力尽きる breathe one's last

□素通りする pass through

□いったん留まる make a short stop

□確執 feud

□第一義 primary purpose

□人間的要素 human characteristics

□排除する exclude

□転戦する moving from one battlefield to another

□集約する aggregate

□〜に仕立てる turn into

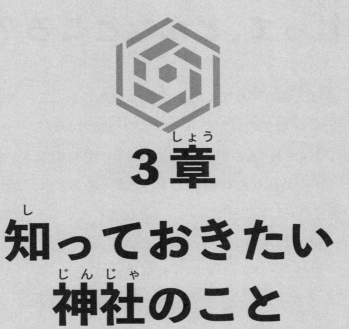

3章

知っておきたい
神社のこと

Chapter 3

What You Should Know
about Shrines

[1] 神社って、どんなところ？

52

古代人は、神は天から降りてくると信じていた。そこで、神が来臨する目印（依り代）を中心に祭場を設けて祭りをおこなったのである。やがて祭場は神の臨時の宿泊所（屋代＝社）とされるようになり、のちに恒久的な施設としての神社に発展した。平安時代初期（西暦927年）にまとめられた「延喜式神名帳」には、国認定の神社（官社）が2861社あったと記されている。小規模の社は、その数十倍あっただろう。

神は「穢れ」を嫌う。そのため神社の境内は神域とされ、入り口としての目印が「鳥居」である。人々がそこから先に足を踏み入れる場合は、穢れを清める必要がある。これを「禊ぎ」といい、「手水舎」で口をすすいで手を洗ったあとに参拝をするのが、神への礼儀とされる。

[1] What Is a Shrine?

Ancient Japanese believed that when a god descended to earth, it left a sign of its visit which could serve as a place of worship. Eventually this place became the temporary lodging for the god, and later developed into a permanent religious facility as a shrine. The *Engi-shiki Jinmyocho*, a list of shrines that was compiled in the early Heian period (927), states that there were 2,861 government-recognized shrines at the time. Counting the smaller shrines, the number was likely ten times larger than that.

The gods dislike defilement. For that reason the precincts of a shrine are considered pure and sacred. The entrance to the shrine is indicated by a *torii* gate. Once a person steps within the gate, he must purify himself or herself. This is called *misogi*. Rinsing out one's mouth and washing one's hands at a basin set in a pavilion is considered proper etiquette before worshipping at a shrine.

Typical Shrine Layout

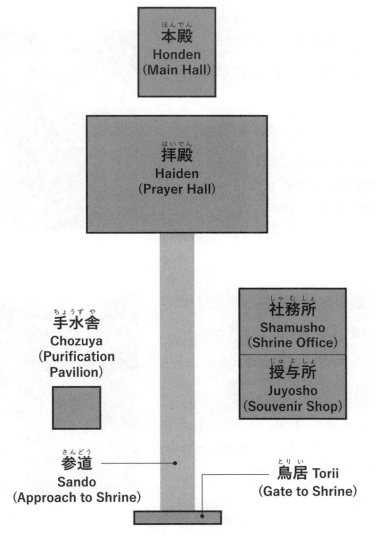

本殿
Honden
(Main Hall)

拝殿
Haiden
(Prayer Hall)

手水舎
Chozuya
(Purification Pavilion)

社務所
Shamusho
(Shrine Office)

授与所
Juyosho
(Souvenir Shop)

参道
Sando
(Approach to Shrine)

鳥居 Torii
(Gate to Shrine)

- □ 来臨する visit
- □ 依り代 *yorishiro*: object to which a spirit is drawn or summoned
- □ 社 shrine
- □ 恒久的な permanent
- □ 施設 facility
- □ 平安時代 Heian period (794–1185)
- □ 延喜式神名帳 a register (927) that records the names of shrines and their gods in Volumes IX and X of the Engishiki (a code of detailed regulations for the enforcement of the Ritsuryo Laws)
- □ 官社 shrines enumerated in the Ritsuryo system in the Jingikan's Registry of Deities
- □ 国認定の government-recognized
- □ 穢れ defilement
- □ 境内 precinct
- □ 神域 sacred area
- □ 鳥居 *torii*: a gateway at the entrance to a Shinto shrine
- □ 足を踏み入れる step within
- □ 禊ぎ purification
- □ 手水舎 purification pavilion
- □ 参拝をする worship

神社によっては、他にさまざまな施設がある。

Depending on the shrine, there are many other possible structures.

| 施設 | Facilities 53 |

鳥居

神域の入り口を示す。二本の柱を上部で結ぶ横木（貫）と、てっぺんに置かれた笠木の組み合わせが基本形。

Torii

This gate marks the entrance to the sacred precinct. Its standard construction consists of two pillars connected by a crossbeam and topped off by a lintel.

手水舎

拝殿に向かう参道の途中にある屋根と柱だけの建物。中に置かれた水盤の水をひしゃくですくって身を清める。

Chozuya, (Temizusha)

This structure, consisting of only of pillars and a roof, is located along the path to the Prayer Hall. Inside is a ladle and basin of water that is used for purification.

社務所

神社の事務一般をおこなう所で、拝殿での正式参拝やご祈祷、お祓いなどの申し込みを受け付ける。

Shamusho

Here is where general administrative affairs are handled, including applications for official prayers, purifications, etc.

授与所

お札、お守り、絵馬、ご朱印、おみくじなどを扱う所。
それぞれの料金を「初穂料」と称する。

Juyosho

Various talismans, votive tablets, good luck charms, etc. can be purchased here. The fee for these items is called the Hatsuho-ryo (First Harvest Fee).

狛犬

祭神を守護し邪気を祓う霊獣像で、一対になって左右に置かれる。厳密には獅子像と狛犬像とされるが、神社によっては狐などの動物像の場合もある。

Komainu

These two beasts, arranged symmetrically on left and right, were meant to protect the enshrined deities and dispel evil spirits. Strictly speaking, they are Chinese lions and Korean dogs, but other animals are sometimes used according to the shrine.

- ☐ 横木 crossbeam
- ☐ 笠木 lintel
- ☐ 拝殿 prayer hall
- ☐ 参道 road approaching a shrine
- ☐ 水盤 basin of water
- ☐ ひしゃく ladle
- ☐ 社務所 shrine office
- ☐ ご祈祷 prayer service
- ☐ お祓い exorcism
- ☐ 授与所 talisman office
- ☐ お札 talisman
- ☐ お守り charm
- ☐ 絵馬 votive picture tablet
- ☐ ご朱印 red seal
- ☐ おみくじ written oracle
- ☐ 初穂料 offering
- ☐ 狛犬 guardian dog, Korean dog
- ☐ 邪気 evil spirit
- ☐ 霊獣 sacred animal
- ☐ 厳密には Strictly speaking
- ☐ 獅子 Chinese lion
- ☐ 一対となる form a pair

狛犬は、口を開けた「阿」像(右)と閉じた「吽」像(左)が一対となる。「阿吽」とは物事の始まりと終わりという意味。

Their open and closed mouths, referred to collectively as *a-un zo*, are the first and last letters of the Sanskrit alphabet, or the beginning and ending of all things.

拝殿

　参拝者が祭神に向かって祈願をする所。神社の中で最も大きな建物で、内部ではご祈祷やお祓いなどの儀式、神前結婚式などがおこなわれる。

　伊勢神宮（三重県）などのように拝殿がない神社の場合は、参拝する場所が定められている。

　また、明治神宮（東京都）などのように2つ（外拝殿・内拝殿）もつ神社もある。

Prayer Hall

Here visitors face in the direction of the enshrined deities and offer their prayers. This is the largest of the buildings in the compound, where rites of devotion and purification are held, in addition to marriage ceremonies etc.

At Ise shrine in Mie prefecture and elsewhere, which have no prayer hall, these rites are conducted at a separate determined location.

At Meiji shrine in Tokyo and elsewhere, there are two prayer halls—an inner and outer.

本殿

　神霊を宿した神体（鏡など）や祭神が祀られている。神社の中心施設だが、参拝者は立ち入ることができない聖域だ。

Main Hall

This is where a god or an object (a mirror etc.) embodying the spirit of a god is enshrined. It is the central facility of the compound, a sacred area inviolable to ordinary shrine visitors.

境内社

神社の境内（敷地）にある社で、祭神以外の神、例えば古くからの地主神（摂社）や大神社の有力神（末社）などが祀られている。

Precinct Shrines

This refers to buildings within the precinct (grounds) of a shrine where deities other than the one to which the shrine is dedicated are enshrined: for example, local tutelary gods with a long history, subordinate shrines, etc.

注連縄

白い紙垂を下げた縄で、神域を示す。ちなみに、横綱が土俵入りのときに腰に締める綱もこの一種で、大相撲が神事とされるゆえんである。

Sacred Shimenawa Rope

This rice rope (*shimenawa*) festooned with white paper streamers encloses an area considered sacred. The fact that Sumo wrestling has a religious origin can be seen in the *shimenawa* worn by the Grand Champion when he enters the ring during the pre-match ceremonies.

- □ 祈願をする pray
- □ 神前結婚式 Shinto wedding ceremony
- □ 神霊 spirit of a deity
- □ 宿す embodying
- □ 神体 sacred body
- □ 聖域 sanctuary
- □ 境内社 precinct shrine
- □ 古くからの地主神 ancient landowner deity
- □ 摂社 regent shrine
- □ 大神社の有力神 influential deity of a major shrine
- □ 末社 subordinate shrine
- □ 注連縄 sacred *shimenawa* rope
- □ 紙垂 paper streamer
- □ 横綱 *yokozuna* (grand champion)
- □ 土俵入り entering the ring during the pre-match ceremonies
- □ 綱 rope
- □ 神事 Shinto ritual

55

［2］参拝のマナー

［2］Proper Manners When Visiting a Shrine

1 鳥居の前で一礼

鳥居から先は神域なので、足を踏み入れる前に「これから立ち入らせていただきます」という挨拶の一礼をする。

1. A Bow before the *Torii*

Beyond the *torii* is the sacred precinct, so before entering, one gives a bow, as if to say, "Pardon me for trespassing on holy ground."

ペットは原則的に入場禁止
As a rule, pets are not permitted.

2 参道は端を歩く

鳥居から拝殿に向かう参道の中央部は「正中」といって、神が通る道。参詣者は、道の両端を歩かなければならない。

2. Walk Down the Side of the Approach to the Prayer Hall

The center of the path leading from the *torii* to the prayer hall is called the *seichu*; this is the part of the approach traveled by the gods. Ordinary visitors must walk along either side of the path.

参道は端を歩く
Walk along the edge of the path.

③ 手水舎に立ち寄る

　参拝者は拝殿に行く前に、穢れた身を清めなければならない。この行為は、黄泉国（死者の国）から逃げ帰ってきたイザナギ（伊邪那岐命）が川でおこなった「禊ぎ」（52ページ）に通じるもので、本来は神社近くの**清流**に入ったり滝に打たれたりした。それを**簡略化した**のが、手水舎の手水を使った「お清め」である。ちなみに神社で葬儀をおこなわないのは、**死穢**（死者の穢れ）を嫌うからである。

3. Stopping by the Purification Pavilion

Before praying to the gods, worshippers must first purify their bodies. This is analogous to Izanagi's purifying himself at a river after escaping from the land of the dead (see page 53). Originally, it was done at a river or stream near the shrine or under a waterfall. An abbreviated version is the purification with water from a basin provided at a purification pavilion (*chozuya*). Incidentally, the reason that funerals are not conducted at shrines is the detestation of the defilement of the dead.

□立ち入る trespass

□一礼をする gives a bow

□正中 *seichu*: the path for the deities

□参詣者 visitor to temple or shrine

□道の両端 both ends of the road

□清流 river or stream

□簡略化した abbreviated

□死穢 death defilement

❹ 手水で身を清める
4. Purification at the Purification Pavilion

56

(1) 軽くおじぎをし、右手でひしゃくを取って水をくむ

(1)

Give a light bow, take a ladle in the right hand and scoop up some water.

(2) 左手を洗う

(2)

Wash the left hand.

(3) ひしゃくを左手に持ち替え、右手を洗う

(3)

Switch the ladle to the left hand and wash the right hand.

(4) ひしゃくを右手に持ち替え、左手に水をためて口をすすぐ。水は飲まないこと

Switch the ladle to the right hand, fill the left hand with water, and rinse out the mouth. Don't drink the water.

(4)

(5) もう一度、左手を洗う

Wash the left hand once more.

(6) ひしゃくを立て、残った水で柄を流し洗いする

(6)

Hold up the ladle and wash the handle off with the remaining water.

(7) ひしゃくを元の場所に戻し、軽くおじぎをする

Return the ladle to its proper place and bow lightly.

(7)

5 拝殿に向かう

お清め後、拝殿に向かう。このとき、参道の中央(正中)を歩かないように注意をする。

拝殿には、漢字の「糸」の字をかたどった白い「紙垂」をつけた藁縄(注連縄)が左右に張られている。このルーツは、アマテラス(天照大神)が天の岩屋から出てきた後で、再び戻れないように封印した「しめ縄(尻久米縄)」とされている(64ページ)。

5. Approaching the Prayer Hall

After purification, one proceeds to the prayer hall, taking care not to walk down the center of the path but staying on the sides.

At the front of the prayer hall is a sacred straw rope (*shimenawa*) with zigzag streamers of white paper on the left and right. This arrangement is said to have its roots in the incident when, after Amaterasu had emerged from the rock cave, she was prevented from reentering by having the entrance blocked by a *shimenawa* called a *shirikumenawa* (see page 65).

□ 柄 handle
□ 藁縄 straw rope
□ 賽銭箱 offertory box
□ ご縁 serendipitous encounter

6 賽銭箱にお金を入れる

拝殿前に置かれた賽銭箱に、お金を入れる。一般的に5円玉が多いのは「ご縁がありますように」との意味合いから。ただし、金額はいくらでもよいが、投げ入れるのはいけない。

6. The Offertory Box

The next step is to put some money in the offertory box placed in front of the prayer hall. A common offering is a five yen coin because "five yen" in Japanese is a homophone for "good luck." Actually, any amount of money is acceptable, but it should not be thrown into the box.

57

7 鈴を鳴らす

拝殿に鈴がある場合は、垂れ下がっている紐を振って鈴を鳴らす。鈴の音で参拝にきたことを神に気づいてもらうためというのは俗説で、本来は「鈴祓い」という魔除けの霊力を高める神事である。

7. Ring the Bell

When the prayer hall has a bell out front, you pull the string to ring the bell. According to tradition, this was meant to call the gods' attention to your arrival, but this is nothing but an old wives' tale. It was originally a ritual for warding off evil and heightening spiritual power.

8 拝礼をする

拝礼の基本動作は、「礼＝おじぎ」と「拍手＝手をたたく」である。正式な拝礼は「二礼二拍手一礼」の作法でおこなう。なお、出雲大社は拝礼の作法が異なる（202ページ）。

8. Worshipping

The act of praying consist basically of bowing and clapping the hands. The authorized method calls for 2 bows, 2 clappings of the hands, and 1 bow. The procedure at the Izumo Oyahshiro is somewhat different, however (see page 203).

【礼】指先と背筋を伸ばし、腰から体を90度に曲げる。両手は膝に当てる（左）。
【拍手】手のひらを丸め、片方の手を少しずらして、両手を打ち合わせる（右）。

[Bowing] Holding the tips of the fingers together and keeping your backbone straight, bend forward from the hips at a 90 degree angle, and place both hands on the knees. (left)
[Clapping the hands] Curve the palms of both hands, shift one hand forward in relation to the other, and hit the two together. (right)

9 祈願をする
き がん

胸元で手を合わせ、頭を下げる。一回の参拝で願いごと
むなもと　　て あ　　　　　あたま さ　　　　　いっかい さんぱい ねが
一つが理想的とされる。
ひと　　りそうてき

9. Praying

Bring the hands together in front
of the chest and bow the head. The
ideal is to pray for one thing at a
time per visit.

10 授与所に立ち寄る
じゅ よ しょ　　 た　 よ

授与所で扱っている「お札」は神霊を家で祀るための
じゅよしょ あつか　　　　　　ふだ　　しんれい いえ まつ
もの。それをコンパクトにして持ち歩けるようにしたのが
も ある
「お守り」である。
まも

10. Visiting the *Juyosho*

Among the talismans sold here, those used for worship in the
home are called *ofuda*; those for carrying on one's person are
called *omamori*.

- 鈴 bell
- 垂れ下がっている hanging down
- 紐 string
- 俗説 nothing but an old wives' tale
- 拝礼 worship
- 拍手 clapping hands
- 作法 procedure
- 胸元 in front of the chest

お札
ふだ
Ofuda
(pictorial or calligraphic invocations)

お守り
まも
Omamori
(talismans for carrying
on one's person)

絵馬
え ま
Ema
(wooden plaques on which worshippers
write wishes or prayers; sometimes
illustrated with depiction of horses)

58

[3] 神社の豆知識
[3] Shrine Trivia

おみくじ

　その人の運勢を記した紙の札。「吉」と「凶」に大別され、神社によってさらに細分化（大・中・小）される。古代人は神の意思をうかがうために動物の骨を焼き、ひび割れの状態で吉凶を判断する「卜占」をおこなっていたが、現代のおみくじのルーツは鎌倉時代初期（12世紀末）に武士が戦の勝機を神にうかがった「籤占」にあるともいわれる。

　おみくじは引いた人の現時点の運勢を占うもので、例えば凶が出たとしても不幸になるといった予言ではない。むしろ書かれているアドバイスを参考にすることで、今日から運気をアップさせることができると受け止めるべきだ。

Omikuji

An *omikuji* is a strip of paper on which a person's fortune is written. They are generally of two types: blessed and cursed. But depending on the shrine, they may be further divided into great, middle, and small. In ancient times people tried to learn the intentions of the gods by burning animal bones and interpreting the cracks produced in the bones. The *omikuji* used today for much the same purpose are said to have their roots in the early 12th-century Kamakura period, when warriors of the time were eager to learn their fate on the battlefield.

　Omikuji tell the present fortune of the person who has received the relevant strip of paper; for example, if you get a cursed or bad luck strip, that is not a prediction for the future. Rather, it is best to follow the accompanying advice on the paper, and thereby see your fortunes take an upward turn.

おみくじには吉凶のほか、願望・健康・仕事・商売・金運・恋愛・結婚・出産・受験など項目ごとの神様のアドバイスが書かれている。和歌を添えたものもある。

Omikuji not only indicate broad categories like "blessed" and "cursed" but also give advice from the gods in narrower fields, such as wishes, health, business, finance, love, childbirth, and school exams. Some are accompanied by a *waka* poem.

吉のくじは持ち帰り、凶のくじは神社の「くじ掛け」に結んで帰ると吉に転じるともいわれる。

A "blessed" *omikuji* can be taken home with one, whereas if a "cursed" *omikuji* is tied to a special wall or wire rack before leaving the shrine, it is transformed into a blessed *omikuji*.

- □ 運勢 fortune
- □ 吉 good luck
- □ 凶 bad luck
- □ 戦の勝機 fate on the battlefield
- □ 運気をアップさせる improve one's luck
- □ 項目ごとの for each item
- □ 和歌を添えた be accompanied by a *waka* poem
- □ 印章 seal
- □ 脇に on the side
- □ 墨書きされる be written in ink

ご朱印

参拝した証しとして参拝者のために押される印章で、お守りやお札と共に神様の分身とされている。印章の上に神社名、脇に参拝日などが墨書きされる。ご朱印用の「ご朱印帳」は授与所にあるが、書店や文房具店で扱うところが増えている。

Red Seals

Red stamps (*goshuin*) are provided to worshippers as evidence that they have visited the shrine. They are considered to be embodiments of the enshrined god much like talismans. At the top is the name of the shrine, and at the side the date when visited etc. in black ink. These can be collected in books available at the *juyosho* or at bookstores and stationery stores.

神社の種類 — Facilities

59

神社は、古代から「**格付け**」がされてきた。最上位は官幣大社で、以下に官幣中社・小社、国幣大社・中社・小社…と続くランキングである。中世には諸国ごとに主な祭神を1か所に集めた総社が設けられ、その下に一宮、二宮、三宮などの神社が制定された。現代の神社の**社号**には、下に示すような格付けの**なごり**がある。

Shrines have been "ranked" since early times. The highest in rank were the major imperial shrines (*kanpei taisha*), followed by the minor imperial shrines (*kanpei chusha, kanpei shosha*), the major national shrines (*kokuhei taisha*), and the minor national shrines (*kokuhei chusha, kokuhei shosha*). In the medieval period (12th to 16th centuries) the various enshrined gods in one province were housed in a specially built shrine (*soja*), under which other shrines were ranked as being of first rank in the province (*ichi-no-miya*), second rank (*ni-no-miya*), etc. In the names of some present-day shrines there are vestiges of the ranking system of bygone years, as can be seen below. (In English these various ranks are often referred to simply as "shrines.")

神宮 Jingu	皇室にゆかりが深い神社の**尊号**で、正式には伊勢神宮（三重県）を指す。伊勢神宮の出張宮の東京大神宮は特例の社号 "Jingu" is a name attached to shrines with a special relationship with the imperial family. Strictly, Jingu refers to Ise Grand Shrine (Ise Jingu) in Mie prefecture. Tokyo Dai-jingu, a branch of Ise Shrine, is an exception to this rule.
宮 Miya	神宮に次ぐ**格式**の神社。天満宮・東照宮などがある This indicates a shrine second in ranking to a *jingu*. Tenmangu and Toshogu are examples. *Gu* here means *miya*.
大社 Taisha	地域の**中核的な**神社。出雲大社（島根県）は「おおやしろ」と読む Indicates a principal shrine of a certain locale. In the case of Izumo Taisha (Izumo Grand Shrine), the characters for "Taisha" are correctly read "Oyashiro," although "Taisha" is common.
神社 Jinja	上記以外の一般の神社 Aside from the above, this is the most common term for a shrine.
社 Sha/ Yashiro	摂社・末社など、神社にゆかりがある神を祀る Indicates a place where a god with deep roots to the shrine is worshipped: for example, *sessha* (auxiliary shrine) and *massha* (branch shrine).

神職 (しんしょく)

The Priesthood

神職の職階は、終戦後に設立（1946年）された宗教法人神社本庁が定めたもので、包括される神社はこれにならっている。ただし、皇室ゆかりの伊勢神宮だけは祭主（女性の皇族出身者）・大宮司・少宮司・禰宜・権禰宜となる。

The hierarchical classification of priests was established by the Association of Shinto Shrines in 1946 after the end of World War II, and aimed at comprehensive adherence by all shrines. However, in the case of Ise Grand Shrine, with its deep connections to the imperial house, the priest hierarchy is *saishu* (a female relative of the imperial family), *daiguji* (chief priest), *shoguji* (assistant priests), *negi* (lower ranking priests), *gonnegi* (assistants to lower ranking priests).

男性の神官の正装
身分によって衣装の色が違う。

Formal costumes of male priests are differentiated by color according to status.

□ 格付け ranking
□ 社号 designation
□ なごり vestige
□ 尊号 precious name
□ ～に次ぐ格式 the second most prestigious after
□ 中核的な principal
□ 神職 priesthood
□ 職階 hierarchical classification
□ 包括される umbrella
□ ～にならう follow
□ 皇室ゆかりの associated with the Imperial Family

神職の職階
Priests' Hierarchy

宮司 Guji
権宮司 Gonguji
▲
禰宜 Negi
権禰宜 Gonnegi

巫女 (みこ)
Miko

古代には神の言葉を伝える役割を与えられた女性を意味したが、現代では神社の女性スタッフの職名になっている。

In ancient times a *miko* was a woman who acted as a medium who communicated the words of a god, but today the word simply refers to one of the shrine's female staff.

| 行事（ぎょうじ） | Events | 60 |

神社でおこなわれる代表的な行事は、以下のとおり。

Here are some of the special events that take place at shrines.

1月	**歳旦祭（さいたんさい）** 1月1日におこなわれる年始を祝う祭り	**January. Saitansai:** Festival held on January 1 to celebrate the beginning of the New Year.
2月	**節分祭（せつぶんさい）** 新春を迎える祭り。2月2日または3日におこなわれる	**February. Setsubunsai:** Festival to welcome the coming of the New Year. Held on the 2nd or 3rd.
2月	**祈年祭（きねんさい）** 五穀豊穣を祈り願う神事。2月17日前後におこなわれる	**February. Kinensai:** A religious rite held in prayer for a bountiful harvest. Held around February 17.
6月	**大祓（おおはらえ）** 夏越の大祓と呼ばれ、6月30日におこなわれる神事	**June. Oharae:** A purification rite (Oharae), also known as Nagoshi no Oharae, that is held on June 30.
8月	**七夕祭（たなばたさい）** 8月7日頃におこなわれ、笹に願いごとを書いた短冊を飾る	**August. Tanabata Festival:** A festival during which one's wishes are written on a strip of paper and tied to bamboo branches; it is held around August 7.
11月	**七五三祝祭（しちごさんしゅくさい）** 子どもの成長を祝い願う祭り。11月15日におこなわれる	**November. Shichigosan Shukusai:** A festival to celebrate the growth and well-being of young children. It is held on November 15.
11月	**新嘗祭（しんじょうさい）** 五穀豊穣を祈り願う祭りで、春の祈年祭と対になる重要神事	**November. Shinjosai:** A rite held in prayer for good harvests. Paired with the Kinensai held in spring, it is an extremely important religious festival.
12月	**煤払祭（すすはらいさい）** 一年間の穢れを払い清めるため、神社の大掃除をおこなう	**December. Susuharaisai:** Literally the "Soot Cleaning Festival," it is meant to cleanse the shrine of the defilement accumulated over the last year.
12月	**大祓（おおはらえ）** 新年を前に、年末におこなわれる祓いの神事	**December. Oharae:** A purification rite held at the end of each year proceeding New Year's.
12月	**除夜祭（じょやさい）** 12月31日の大祓後の夜におこなわれる神事	**December. Joyasai:** A religious rite held on the night of December 31 after the Oharae.

初詣
（はつもうで）

新年の最初の神社参りで、一年の無事を祈願する。一般的には正月三が日（1月1日〜3日）だが、関東では7日まで、関西では15日まで、地方によっては20日までというように期間にばらつきがある。

Hatsumode

The first visit to a shrine in the New Year, when prayers are offered for a safe and prosperous coming year, is call *Hatsumode*. It generally takes place from January 1 to January 3, but in the Kanto region this period is extended to the 7th and in the Kansai region to the 15th. In some areas it lasts as long as the 20th, showing that there is considerable variety depending on the locality.

お正月は、家に年神様が訪れるとされる。年末に大掃除をし、門松を立て、注連飾りを準備するのは、年神様を迎えるため。お供えの餅には神力が宿り、それを食べることで年神様のパワーをいただく。

During New Year's it is said that homes are visited by the Year God (Toshigami). It is to welcome this god that the house is thoroughly cleaned at the end of the year, a decorative pine-gate (*kadomatsu*) is erected, and a decorative sacred rope (*shimekazari*) is set up. The rice cakes (*kagamimochi*) that are offered are said to embody the deity's spirit and transfer that power to those who eat the cakes.

門松
Kadomatsu

注連飾り
Shimekazari

鏡餅
Kagamimochi

61

初宮参り

生後1か月の赤ちゃんを連れて、お参りする。両
親と父方の祖母が**同伴する**風習がある。

初宮参り
Hatsu Miyamairi

Hatsu Miyamairi

This (the First Shrine Visit) refers to the practice of taking a one-month-old baby to a shrine for the fist time. It is also customary for the paternal grandmother to accompany the child and its parents.

七五三詣

11月15日に、3歳、5歳、7歳になった子どもを
連れて、お参りする。神様のパワーが入った**飴**など
が**授与される**。

七五三
Shichi-go-san

Shichi-go-san

On November 11, children who have reached the ages of 3, 5, or 7 (*shichi-go-san*) are taken to pray at a shrine. There they receive special candy which symbolizes healthy growth and longevity.

神前結婚式

ルーツは、大正天皇が皇太子のとき(1900年)、皇居でおこなわれた結婚式と
される。その後、神社で**挙式**を受け付けるようになり、今や神職を派遣してホ
テルなどでおこなう神前結婚式も盛んになった。

Shinto Weddings

The first Shinto wedding is said to have taken place in 1900 at the imperial palace when Emperor Taisho was crown prince. Thereafter shrines began to accept applications for wedding ceremonies, and now it is common for priests to be dispatched to hotels and other sites to conduct wedding rites.

祭り

　古来、日本人は日常を「ケ(穢れ)」、非日常を「ハレ(晴れ)」と考えていた。神社の祭りは地域にとっての「ハレの日」で、このときは神様を聖域から外へ連れ出し、その霊力を地域にみなぎらせようとした。祭りで神様の乗り物(神輿や山車)を揺り動かすのは、神魂のパワーを高めるためだ。

Matsuri

From ancient times the Japanese have divided days into those that were "defiled" (*kegare*) and those that were "clear" (*hare*). For the local community the shrine's *matsuri* (festivals) were held on a clear day when the enshrined god was taken out of the sacred precinct into the outside world, where its power could permeate the surrounding area. The vehicles conveying the deity during the festival—the *mikoshi* (portable shrines) and *dashi* (floats)—were shaken by the parishioners to stimulate the god to a heightened degree of spiritual power.

- □初宮参り Baby's First Shrine Visit
- □同伴する accompany
- □飴 Japanese candy
- □授与される receive
- □挙式 wedding ceremony
- □みなぎらせる fill
- □神輿 portable shrine
- □山車 festival float
- □揺り動かす sway

神田祭　大小200もの神輿が練り歩く

Kanda Matsuri: An assorted parade of 200 portable shrines and floats

62

[4] 神にされた人物

　1～2章で詳述したように、日本神道の聖典ともされる『古事記』と『日本書紀』は、天上界の最高神アマテラス（天照大神）を天皇家の祖神であるとする。そして、天上の神々は不死だが、地上の神々は死を免れない、つまり**人間に限りなく近い存在**として描いている。したがって、日本の神々を語る場合は、天上界と地上界の神概念が異なることを**踏まえる**必要がある。

　神社では「穢れ」が災いをもたらすと、**禁忌**にしている。その**究極**が「死穢」と「**血穢**」である。前者は文字どおり死の穢れで、特に怨念を抱いて死んだ人間は悪霊になって**天災や疫病**をもたらすと考えられた。それを封じこめる役割を与えられた神社があったのは、今や定説である。一方、後者は主に女性の出産にまつわる出血を意味する。神話でも、出産時の悲劇が語られている（100ページ、106ページ）。

　以下に、**歴史上の人物**が死後に**神**として**祀**られた例を紹介する。

[4] People who Became Gods

As discussed in chapters 1 and 2, according to the sacred books of Shinto, the *Kojiki* and *Nihon Shoki*, the principal god in the heavenly realm is Amaterasu, who is also the guardian goddess of the Japanese imperial family. However, while the heavenly gods were immortal, the gods of the earthly realm were mortal; that is, they were depicted as being all too human. Thus when speaking of the gods of Japan, it must be kept in mind that the concept of "god" is different according to whether one is speaking of heavenly or earthly gods.

At Shinto shrines it is thought that defilement gives rise to misfortune, and for this reason it is considered taboo. The extreme example of this is the defilement that comes from death or blood. Particularly in the case of the former, it was thought that when a person died bearing revengeful feelings, the dead person would turn into an evil spirit and cause disasters and plagues. It was commonly thought that it was the role of the shrine to control these phenomena. In the case of blood, the most common example was the loss of blood accompanying childbirth. The myths themselves contain many tragic tales concerning childbirth (see pages 101 and 107).

Below I will give some examples of historical figures who have been raised to the status of gods.

□詳述する detail
□人間に限りなく近い存在 all too human
□踏まえる take into account
□禁忌 taboo
□血穢 blood defilement
□天災 natural disaster
□疫病 epidemic
□歴史上の人物 historical figure
□神として祀られる deified

菅原 道真
すがわらの みちざね

鎮魂のために神として祀られる
ちんこん　　　　　　かみ　　　　　まつ

菅原道真（845－903）は学者の家系で、幼少から優秀
すがわらのみちざね　　　　　　　　　　　がくしゃ　かけい　　　　　　ようしょう　ゆうしゅう
だった。やがて59代宇多天皇の側近として出世をし55
　　　　　　　　　　　だいうだてんのう　そっきん　　　　　しゅっせ
歳で右大臣になった。しかし、それを妬んだ藤原時平の
さい　うだいじん　　　　　　　　　　　ねた　　　ふじわらのときひら
讒言で九州・太宰府に左遷され、失意のうちに57歳で
ざんげん　きゅうしゅう　だざいふ　させん　　　　しつい　　　　　　さい
死去。
しきょ

死後、京都では疫病の流行、洪水や大火などに加え、時平（39歳）やその親族
しご　きょうと　　えきびょう　りゅうこう　こうずい　たいか　　　　くわ　ときひら　さい　　　　しんぞく
の若死といった異変が起きる。極め付きは落雷事件（930年）だ。落雷は天皇の御
わかじに　　　　　いへん　お　　　きわ　つ　　　らくらいじけん　　ねん　　　らくらい　てんのう　ご
所を襲い、多くの死傷者が出た。京都の人々は、これらを道真の祟りとした。
しょ　おそ　　おお　　ししょうしゃ　で　　きょうと　ひとびと　　　　　　　みちざね　たた
その霊を鎮め、都の守護神として祀る神社（現在の北野天満宮、190ページ）が造営
れい　しず　みやこ　しゅごしん　　　まつ　じんじゃ　げんざい　きたのてんまんぐう　　　　　　ぞうえい
されたのは、死後44年（947年）。その40年後、一條天皇が「北野天満大自在
しご　ねん　　ねん　　　　　　　　　　ねんご　いちじょうてんのう　きたのてんまんだいじざい
天神」という神号を与えた。
てんじん　　　　しんごう　あた

安倍 晴明
あべの せいめい

陰陽師の祖神として祀られる
おんみょうじ　おやがみ　　　　　まつ

安倍晴明（921－1005）は、朝廷に仕えた陰陽師の始祖
あべのせいめい　　　　　　　　　ちょうてい　つか　　おんみょうじ　しそ
とされる。いわば国家公務員として、天文・暦・時刻な
　　　　　　こっかこうむいん　　　　　てんもん　こよみ　じこく
どを担当する陰陽寮という役所に勤務し、主に天文の変
　たんとう　おんようりょう　やくしょ　きんむ　おも　てんもん　へん
化で吉凶を占う部門を担当した。その予知能力の高さか
か　きっきょう　うらな　ぶもん　たんとう　　　　よちのうりょく　たか
ら、皇室のみならず貴族たちからも一目置かれる存在だった。のちに子孫は土御
こうしつ　　　　　きぞく　　　　　　　いちもくお　　　そんざい　　　　　　しそん　つちみ
門家を興し、近世には全国の陰陽師を支配する宗家となった。
かどけ　おこ　きんせい　ぜんこく　おんみょうじ　しはい　そうけ

Sugawara No Michizane
Worshipped as a God to Pacify an Angry Spirit

Sugawara no Michizane (845–903) was born into a scholarly family and an excellent student from an early age. Eventually he became aide to the 59th emperor, Uta, and at the age of 55 was appointed Minister of the Right. However, this aroused the jealousy of Fujiwara no Tokihira, whose slander caused Michizane to be relegated to provincial post in Dazaifu, Kyushu. He died there at the age of 57 in the depths of despair.

After Michizane's death, calamity struck in various ways: a plague broke out in Kyoto; there was flooding and fires; and Tokihira died at the age of 39, as well as younger members of his family. The ultimate event was the lightning incident of 930. The imperial palace was struck by lightning, resulting in many deaths. The people of Kyoto attributed this to the curse of Michizane. In 947, 44 years after Michizane's death, a shrine (present Kitano Tenmangu; see page 191) was erected as a means of pacifying his spirit and as a guardian of the city. Forty years later, Emperor Ichijo assigned Michizane the divine name of Kitano Tenman Dai Jizai Tenjin.

- □ 側近 close associate
- □ 右大臣 Minister of the Right
- □ 妬む envy
- □ 讒言 calumny
- □ ～に左遷される be demoted to
- □ 失意のうちに in despair
- □ 極め付き the worst case
- □ 落雷 lightning strike
- □ 神号 divine title

Abe no Seimei
Worshipped as the Guardian God of Spiritual Advisors

Abe no Seimei (921–1005) was the first spiritual advisor (*onmyoji*) to serve the imperial court. A type of civil servant, he worked in the Bureau of *Yin* and *Yang*, where he was in charge of astronomy, the calendar, time, and other matters, specializing in foretelling the future by the movement of the celestial bodies. His outstanding ability drew the attention not only of the imperial family but of the court nobility. His later descendants founded the Tsuchimikado family, which was a dominant force in the field nationwide in the early modern period.

- □ 陰陽師 *yin-yang* master
- □ 陰陽寮 Bureau of *Yin* and *Yang*
- □ 吉凶を占う divine good and bad fortune
- □ 一目置かれる be respected
- □ 興す establish
- □ 宗家 head family

晴明を神に祀り上げたのは、**後世の陰陽師やその影響を受けた庶民たち**である。なかでも12世紀前半に編纂された『今昔物語集』には晴明の超能力を示す**説話**があることから、庶民の中に晴明信仰が広まっていたことがうかがえる。

晴明を祀る神社は、京都(上京区)・大阪(阿倍野区)・和歌山(龍神村)などにある。

平 将門

1000年以上経った今も怖れられている祟り

平将門(?−940)は、菅原道真(前出)、75代崇徳天皇(のち上皇)と共に「日本三大怨霊」とされる。

50代桓武天皇の子孫で、祖父が国司として赴任した上総国(現在の千葉県)で育ち、やがて京都に出て役人になった。しかし思うような出世ができずに地元に帰るが、親族との**争いに巻きこまれる**。それに勝利した将門は関東諸国へと勢力を伸ばし、天皇に対抗して「新皇」を自称するが、2か月ほどで**討伐された**。

死後、首は京都でさらされたが、**ほどなく関東のほうへ飛んで行った**という。**首が落ちてきた伝承地**の一つが東京の大手町で、現在も「首塚」がのこる。これを壊そうとすると祟りがあるとされ、将門は近くの神田神社(168ページ)で祭神として祀られている。

What raised Seimei to the status of a god were the subsequent generations of spiritual advisors and the common people who were influenced by them. In particular, from a tale appearing in the *Konjaku monogatari-shu* (Anthology of Tales from the Past; compiled in the late 12th century), which deals with Seimei's supernatural powers, we can see that the number of believers in Seimei had spread widely. Shrines dedicated to Seimei include those in Kyoto (Kamigyo-ku), Osaka (Abeno-ku), and Wakayama (Ryujin-mura).

□ 後世の later generations of
□ 庶民たち common people
□ 説話 legendary tale

Taira no Masakado
The Curse Still Feared 1,000 Years Later

Taira no Masakado, Sugawara Michizane, and the 75th emperor Sutoku are known as the Three Great Vengeful Spirits of Japan.

A descendant of the 50th emperor Kanmu, Masakado grew up in Kazusa province where his grandfather was serving as governor. Later, in Kyoto, he became a civil servant. However, when his prospects for advancement didn't pan out, he returned to Kazusa, where he became entangled in a family feud. Masakado emerged victorious and extended his influence into the Kanto region. Vying with the emperor, he dubbed himself the "new emperor." However, in a mere two months time he was suppressed.

Following his death, his severed head was put on public display in Kyoto, but shortly thereafter it is said to have flown off to the Kanto region. One of the places where the head is said to have come to earth is Otemachi in Tokyo; a memorial still stands there today. Whenever there is talk of removing it, the curse of Masakado is brought up. Masakado is worshipped as a god at the nearby Kanda Shrine (see page 169).

□ 上皇 retired emperor
□ 国司 provincial governor
□ ～として赴任した be posted as
□ 争いに巻きこまれる become embroiled in a dispute
□ 討伐される be killed in battle
□ 首 severed head
□ さらされる put on public display
□ ほどなく shortly thereafter
□ 首が落ちてきた伝承地 the places where his head is said to have landed
□ 首塚 head mound

豊臣 秀吉

66

死の翌年に朝廷から豊国大明神の神号を授与

豊臣秀吉(1537–1598)は、戦国時代に下層民から仕官をし、大名になって天下統一を果たし、太政大臣という最高の官位を得た。死後、朝廷から豊国大明神の神号が授与され、1599年に京都に豊国神社が創建された。翌年、秀吉がかつて城主だった長浜(滋賀県)にも豊国神社が創建され、ここには事代主大神・加藤清正・木村重成も併せて祀られた。

豊臣家は秀吉の死後17年ほどで徳川家康によって滅ぼされたが、その前後に小松島(徳島県)と金沢(石川県)に豊国神社が創建されている。後者は、加賀藩主の前田家が密かに秀吉像を祀っていた社に由来する。大阪の豊國神社は1879年、名古屋の豊国神社は1885年の創建。

徳川 家康

67

最盛期には700社あった東照宮の祭神

徳川家康(1542–1616)は、戦国の世を生き抜いて250年にわたる泰平の世を築いた江戸幕府の創始者である。

死後、遺言に従って遺体は久能山(静岡県)に葬られ、東照社が創建された。朝廷はこの神社に東照大権現という神号を贈り、家康を祭神とした。

Toyotomi Hideyoshi
Given a Divine Name a Year after Death

Toyotomi Hideyoshi (1537–98) was born into a peasant family in the period of Warring States (1467–1615), attained a government position, became a feudal lord and unified the nation, finally achieving the ultimate rank of Chancellor of the Realm. After his death the imperial court awarded him the divine name of Toyokuni Daimyojin, and in 1599 the Toyokuni shrine was erected in his commemoration in Kyoto. In the following year, the Hokoku shrine was erected where Hideyoshi's castle once stood in Nagahama, Shiga prefecture, where he is worshipped as a god together with Kotoshironushi, Kato Kiyomasa, and Kimura Shigenari.

About 17 years after the death of Hideyoshi, the Toyotomi family was utterly destroyed by Tokugawa Ieyasu. Around the same time Toyokuni shrines dedicated to Hideyoshi were built in Komatsushima (Tokushima prefecture) and Kanazawa (Ishikawa prefecture). The latter has its roots in the shrine housing a statue of Hideyoshi that the Maeda clan, lords of the Kaga domain, had secretly created as an object of worship. The Hokoku shrine in Osaka dates to 1879, and the Toyokuni shrine in Nagoya to 1885.

□戦国時代 Warring States period
□下層民 lower class
□仕官をする enter the service of a lord
□太政大臣 Grand Minister of State
□創建される be built
□〜も併せて also
□滅ぼされる be overthrown
□その前後に around that time

Tokugawa Ieyasu
As Many as of 700 Toshogu Shrines Dedicated to Ieyasu

Tokugawa Ieyasu (1542–1616) was the founder of the Edo shogunate, which brought an end to the period of Warring States and established an era of peace that lasted some 250 years.

After his death, according to his will, his remains were buried on Mount Kuno (Shizuoka prefecture) and a shrine (Toshosha) erected in his honor. The imperial court assigned the shrine the divine name Tosho Daigongen, "Great Gongen, Light of the East," making Ieyasu the enshrined deity.

□泰平の世 peaceful era
□遺言 will
□葬られる be laid to rest

この神号は神仏習合の影響を受けたもので、仏である薬師如来がこの世に神という仮の姿で現れたことを意味する。一周忌には、日光(栃木県)に創建された東照大権現で遷座祭りが挙行された。

1645年、朝廷は東照大権現に格式の高い「宮」号を贈り、以来、社名は東照宮となった。幕府の威光を背景に東照宮は全国各地に700社ほど造営されたが、現存するのは約130社とされる。

西郷 隆盛

高潔な人徳を庶民が神徳に高めた

68

西郷隆盛(1828 – 1877)は、明治維新の最大の功労者とされたが、政府内での対立により故郷の薩摩(鹿児島県)に帰る。やがて新政権に不満を抱く旧士族たちに担がれて武装蜂起を指導し、西南戦争となった。1877年9月、官軍の総攻撃で薩摩軍は全滅し、西郷は城山で自刃。2年後、西郷の遺体の仮埋葬地に九州各地に散在していた薩摩軍の遺骨2000余りを集めて西郷の号にちなんだ南洲墓地が造られ、その隣に参拝所が設けられた。

西郷が名誉回復を果たしたのは死後十数年後で、参拝所は1922年に南洲神社として認定された。南洲神社は酒田(山形県)、都城(宮崎県)、沖永良部島(鹿児島県)にもある。

This divine name was formed under the syncretism of Buddhism and Shinto, which meant that the buddha Yakushi appeared on earth in the form of a Shinto god. On the first anniversary of Ieyasu's death, the present-day shrine at Nikko (Tochigi prefecture) was built, and a festival held there to celebrate the newly enshrined deity.

It was in 1645 that the imperial court awarded the shrine the high rank of *gu-go*, officially making the name of the shrine "Toshogu." Backed by the prestige of the shogunate, there were eventually 700 shrines named Toshogu built throughout the country, but today that number has shrunken to about 130.

□神仏習合 syncretism of Buddhism and Shinto

□仏 Buddha

□薬師如来 Bhaisajyaguru (buddha able to cure all ills)

□仮の姿 manifestation

□一周忌 first anniversary of one's death

□遷座祭り enshrinement ceremony

□挙行された be held

□格式の高い prestigious

□造営された be constructed

Saigo Takamori
Human Integrity Raised to Godly Status by the Common People

Saigo Takamori (1828–77) was one of the greatest contributors to the Meiji Restoration, but due to internal conflict within the new Meiji government he returned to his home in Satsuma (Kagoshima prefecture). There he became the leader of former samurais who were dissatisfied with the government, which eventually led to an armed uprising known as the Seinan War or Satsuma Rebellion. In September 1877 the Satsuma forces were destroyed by the government troops and Takamori took his own life by committing *seppuku* at Shiroyama. Two years later, the remains of more than 2,000 Satsuma soldiers, which had been scattered throughout Kyushu, were assembled and buried in Saigo's temporary grave, which was newly named the Nanshu Cemetery after Saigo's pen name "Nanshu." Next to the cemetery was built a place for offering prayers.

Takamori won back his good name several dozens of years later when, in 1922, the cemetery was officially recognized as the Nanshu shrine. There are also Nanshu shrines in Sakata (Yamagata prefecture), Miyakonojo (Miyazaki prefecture), and Okinoerabu island (Kagoshima prefecture).

□明治維新 Meiji Restoration

□功労者 contributor

□対立 conflict

□旧士族 former samurai

□担がれる be carried by

□武装蜂起 armed rebellion

□官軍 government troops

□総攻撃 final assault

□自刃 ritual suicide

□遺骨 remains

□号 pen name

□認定される be recognized

明治天皇

天皇を神に祀り上げた明治新政府

　122代明治天皇(1852–1912)は、明治維新後の国民に「現人(御)神」の存在を知らしめることになった。この世に人間の姿で現れた神という意味だが、その背景には「天孫降臨」の神話(94ページ)がある。それまで天皇は「お上」と呼ばれていた。いわば天上の存在というニュアンスの呼称だが、「神」という直截的な表現ではなく、その呼称には人間としての親近感すらおぼえる。

　実は、天皇を神として宣揚しなければならなかったのは、明治新政府である。近代国家への転換を図った新政府は、中央集権のためのイデオロギーとして国家神道を選択し、その要として天皇を神に祀り上げたというべきだろう(170ページ)。

Emperor Meiji
The New Government Deifies Emperor Meiji

It was after the Meiji Restoration of 1868 that the people of Japan first learned that the emperor was a *arahitogami*—that is, a god in human form. This notion was supported by the myth describing the descent of heavenly gods to earth (see page 95). Until that time the emperor was simply referred to as Okami (His Majesty; literally, Honorable Aboveness). While Okami can be said to suggest an existence from above, it does not directly refer to a "god." Rather "Okami" has a feeling of human intimacy.

The Meiji government had a need to promote the godliness of the emperor. As part of its plans to convert Japan into a modern nation and to concentrate all power in the central government, the Meiji government chose to make Shinto a state religion as part of its political ideology. This necessarily called for the deification of the emperor (see page 171).

□現人（御）神 living god

□天上の存在 heavenly being

□直截的な straightforward

□親近感 closeness

□宣揚する promote

□転換を図る aim to transform

□中央集権 concentration of power

□イデオロギー ideology

□国家神道 state Shinto

□要 keystone

4章
代表的な神社

Chapter 4

Representative Shrines

東日本
East Japan

❶ 鹽竈神社 p.158

❻ 氷川神社 p.166

❷ 日光東照宮 p.160

❺ 秩父神社 p.164

⓯ 諏訪大社 p.176

❸ 鹿島神宮 p.162

❹ 香取神宮 p.162

⓮ 富士山本宮浅間大社 p.174

❼ 東京大神宮 p.166

❽ 神田神社 p.168

⓭ 秋葉山本宮秋葉神社 p.174

❾ 湯島天満宮 p.168

❿ 明治神宮 p.170

⓬ 鶴岡八幡宮 p.172

⓫ 水天宮 p.172

❶ 鹽竈神社(宮城)

古代から東北地方随一の格式を誇る

　鹽竈(塩釜)とは、塩の採取のために海水を煮立てる釜のこと。古来、塩は人間に不可欠な養分とされてきた。神社の主祭神である塩土老翁は人々に塩づくりを教えたとされ、『古事記』では海神の化身として現れて主人公を助ける(104ページ)。創建年代は不明だが、陸奥国一之宮として古くから崇敬を集めてきた。

【主なご利益】産業発展、海上安全、安産守護、延命長寿など

【特色など】拝殿は二つで別宮拝殿に主祭神、左右拝殿にタケミカヅチ神・フツヌシ神が祀られている

【所在地】宮城県塩竈市一森山

鹽竈神社　参道
しおがまじんじゃ　さんどう
The approach to Shiogama Jinja

❶ Shiogama Jinja (Miyagi)
The Highest Ranked Shrine in Tohoku since Ancient Times

A *shiogama* is a cauldron in which seawater is boiled to produced salt, a substance that has been considered essential for life since ancient times. The shrine's principal god is Shiotsuchioji, who is said to have taught human beings how to make salt. In the *Kojiki* he appears as a manifestation of the God of the Sea and saves the protagonist in a time of need (see page 105). The exact date of the erection of the temple is unclear, but it has been venerated from old as one of the "first shrines" (*ichi no miya*) of Mutsu province (present Fukushima, Miyagi, Iwate, and Aomori prefectures).

◆ **Object of Prayers**: business prosperity, safe childbirth, long life, and others.

◆ **Features**: There are two prayer halls. One is the detached sanctuary (*betsugu*) in which the principal deity is enshrined. The other consists of the left and right sanctuaries in which Takemikazuchi and Futsunushi are enshrined.

◆ **Location**: Ichimoriyama, Shiogama city, Miyagi prefecture.

□鹽竈（塩釜）salt kiln
□採取 collection
□釜 caldron
□不可欠な養分 essential nutrient
□化身 incarnation
□崇敬を集める be venerated
□ご利益 main benefits

71

❷ 日光東照宮（栃木）

世界文化遺産に登録された絢爛豪華な社殿

江戸幕府の初代将軍・徳川家康を祭神（東照大権現）とする（150ページ）。久能山（静岡）・上野（東京）など各地にある「東照宮」の総本社である。現在にのこる**絢爛豪華な社殿群は、孫の三代将軍・家光によって築造されたもの**（1636年）。1999年、**世界文化遺産「日光の社寺」の一つとして登録された**。

【**主なご利益**】出世、学業成就、商売繁盛、家内安全など

【**特色など**】本殿と拝殿を石の間でつなぐ配置を「権現造り」という

【**所在地**】栃木県日光市山内

【**陽明門**】本殿（国宝）の入り口となる陽明門（国宝）は、竜や獅子など500余りの彫刻で飾り立てられている

東照宮の建物は金箔や漆などによる鮮やかな彫刻が施され、総数5000を超える。2013年に本殿・石の間・拝殿と陽明門の修理が始まり、2019年3月に終了した

日光東照宮　陽明門

Nikko Toshogu Yomeimon gate

❷ Nikko Toshogu (Tochigi)

A Spectacular Shrine Designated a UNESCO World Heritage Site

This shrine takes as its enshrined deity the first shogun of the Tokugawa shogunate, Tokugawa Ieyasu, whose divine name is Tosho Daigongen (see page 151). There are other Toshogu shrines throughout the country, such as the ones at Kunozan (Shizuoka pref.) and Ueno (Tokyo), of which Nikko Toshogu is the head shrine. The splendid complex surviving today was constructed by Ieyasu's grandson, the third Tokugawa shogun, Iemitsu, in 1636. In 1999 it was listed as a UNESCO World Heritage Site.

- **Object of Prayers**: success in life, academic achievement, family well-being, and others.

- **Features**: The main hall and the prayer hall are connected by a "stone room"; this type of layout is known as the *gongen* style.

- **Location**: Sannai, Nikko city, Tochigi prefecture.

- **Yomeimon gate**: The Yomeimon (National Treasure) leads to the main hall (National Treasure). It is adorned with dragons, Chinese lions, and more than 500 other sculptures.
  The buildings of the Toshogu are embellished with gold and silver foil and lacquer, totaling more than 5,000 decorations. Repair work on the main hall, stone room, prayer hall, and Yomeimon began in 2013 and was completed in March 2019.

□ 総本社 head shrine
□ 絢爛豪華な magnificent
□ 社殿 main shrine building
□ 築造された be constructed
□ 世界文化遺産 World Heritage Site
□ 石の間 stone chamber
□ 金箔 gold leaf
□ 漆 lacquer
□ 施される be decorated

72

❸鹿島神宮（茨城）

日本建国・武道の神タケミカヅチを祀る

創建は初代・神武天皇の世と伝わる。祭神は武甕槌大神で、アマテラス（天照大神）に命じられて地上に降り、神剣の霊力でオオクニヌシ（大国主神）に国譲りを迫った天神である（84ページ）。そのため、「建国の神」「武神」として天皇家や鎌倉・江戸幕府に尊崇されてきた。12年ごとの「御船祭」は、水上の一大祭典だ。

【主なご利益】武道上達、海上守護、安産、延命長寿など

【特色など】全国に約500社ある鹿島神社の総本社

【所在地】茨城県鹿嶋市宮中

❹香取神宮（栃木）

今も武道家の聖地とされる関東屈指の古社

近くの鹿島神宮と共に東国三社の一社として、古代から崇敬されてきた。祭神の経津主大神（香取神）は、鹿島神宮の祭神タケミカヅチと共に天降りをした武神である。神宮は約600年前から伝承されてきた香取神道流という武術道場としても知られ、武道家のパワースポットだ。祭神は、春日大社（奈良）などにも勧請されている。

【主なご利益】勝運、海上守護、交通安全、産業振興、安産など

【特色など】全国に約400社ある香取神社の総本社

【所在地】千葉県香取市香取

❸ Kashima Jingu (Ibaraki)

Dedicated to Takemikazuchi, Nation Founder and God of Martial Arts

The founding of the temple is said to have taken place in the reign of Emperor Jinmu, the first emperor. The enshrined deity is Takemikazuchi. As a heavenly god he was ordered by Amaterasu to descend to the earth, where, with his magical divine sword, he pressed Okuninushi to relinquish his land (*kuniyuzuri*; see page 85). Thus, as a founder of the nation and as a god of martial arts, Takemikazuchi was highly revered by the imperial family and the Kamakura and Edo shogunates. The Mifune Festival, held partially on water once every 12 years, is a magnificent celebration of the first order.

- ◆ **Object of Prayers**: improvement in martial arts, maritime safety, safe childbirth, long life, and others.

- ◆ **Features**: The head temple of approximately 500 Kashima Shrines throughout the country.

- ◆ **Location**: Kyuchu, Kashima city, Ibaraki prefecture.

□〜の世 reign of
□尊崇される be revered

❹ Katori Jingu (Tochigi)

One of the Oldest Shrines in Kanto, Even Now Sacred Ground to Martial Artists

Katori Jinju, together with nearby Kashima Jingu, has long been revered as one of the three great shrines of the Kanto region. The enshrined deity is Futsunushi, the god of martial arts who descended from heaven with the enshrined Takemikazuchi of Kashima Jingu. Katori Jingu is known for its *dojo* of traditional martial arts (Katori Shinto-ryu), with a history of some 600 years, and is considered a power spot by martial artists. The enshrined deity can also be worshipped at temples such as Kasuga Taisha (Nara).

- ◆ **Object of Prayers**: luck in competition, maritime safety, traffic safety, industrial promotion, and others.

- ◆ **Features**: Head temple of approximately 400 Katori Shrines throughout Japan.

- ◆ **Location**: Katori, Katori city, Chiba prefecture.

□伝承される be handed down
□武道家 martial artist
□勧請される be enshrined

73

❺秩父神社(埼玉)

世界無形文化遺産になった例大祭「秩父夜祭」

約2100年前の創建と伝えられる古社で、知知夫国の総鎮守として現在に至る。初代国造に任命された知知夫彦命が、10代前の祖神・八意思兼命(62ページ)を祀ったことに始まるとされる。この二柱に加え、創成神・天之御中主神(48ページ)と秩父宮雍仁親王を祭神としている。現存の社殿は、徳川家康の寄進による。

【主なご利益】学問上達、厄除開運、産業振興、長寿、眼病平癒など

【特色など】武甲山は秩父神社の神体山とされる

【所在地】埼玉県秩父市番場町

【秩父夜祭】例年12月3日におこなわれ、祭神の一柱のアメノミナカヌシ(妙見様)にちなんだ祭礼。典雅な神代神楽、勇壮な屋台囃子、豪華な笠鉾・屋台の曳き回し、盛大な打ち上げ花火の競演が繰り広げられる。2016年、世界無形文化遺産に登録された

秩父夜祭

Chichibu's Night Festival

❺ Chichibu Jinja (Saitama)

The Shrine's Annual Night Festival Has Been Designated an Intangible Heritage of Humanity

An ancient shrine said to have been established about 2,100 years ago, it is the tutelary shrine dedicated to all the gods in Chichibu province. Its roots are said to lie in the order of an early magistrate (Kuninomiyatsuko) calling for the enshrinement of the god Chichibu, whose grandfather was the god Yagokoroomoikane of ten generations earlier (see page 63). In addition to these two gods, the enshrined gods also include the creator god Amenominakanushi (see page 49) and Chichibu-no-miya Yasuhito Shinno (Prince Yasuhito). The present buildings were made possible by contributions from Tokugawa Ieyasu.

- **Object of Prayers**: academic improvement, warding off evil and attracting good fortune, promotion of business, longevity, healing of eye diseases, and others.

- **Features**: Mount Buko is the embodiment of the gods (*shintaizan*) of Chichibu Shrine.

- **Location**: Banba-machi, Chichibu city, Saitama prefecture.

- **Chichibu's Night Festival**: Held annually on December 3, this festival is associated with the enshrined god Amenominakanushi (also known as Myoken-sama). There are elegant *kagura* dances, music with multiple drums, gorgeous umbrella-halberd featured floats, float parades, and spectacular competitions of fireworks. In 2016 it was designated an Intangible Cultural Heritage.

☐ 総鎮守 main tutelary shrine

☐ 現在に至る continue to this day

☐ 任命される be appointed

☐ 現存の extant

☐ 平癒 healing

☐ ～にちなんだ associated with

☐ 典雅な elegant

☐ 勇壮な majestic

☐ 屋台囃子 festival float music

☐ 笠鉾 halberd float

☐ 屋台の曳き回し float procession

☐ 盛大な打ち上げ花火の競演 spectacular fireworks display

☐ 繰り広げられる be performed

☐ 世界無形文化遺産 World Intangible Cultural Heritage

74

❻ 氷川神社(埼玉)

縁結びの神社として古代から崇敬される

社記によると創建は約2400年以上も前で、東国平定にやってきたヤマトタケル(116ページ)も参拝したと伝わる。祭神は須佐之男命・稲田姫命の夫婦神(72ページ)と大己貴命(74ページ)。大己貴命は、出雲大社の主祭神のオオクニヌシである。このことから古来、縁結びや家庭円満の神社として知られてきた。

【主なご利益】縁結び、子授け、家庭円満、商売繁盛、稲作守護など

【特色など】埼玉・東京・神奈川に約280社ある氷川神社の総本社

【所在地】さいたま市大宮区高鼻町

❼ 東京大神宮(東京)

神前結婚式を創始した「東京のお伊勢さま」

明治天皇の裁可で、東京における伊勢神宮の遥拝殿として創建された(1880年)。主祭神は天照皇大神と豊受大神で、造化三神(48ページ)と倭比賣命(116ページ)も祭神になっている。日比谷大神宮、飯田橋大神宮と社名を変え、現社名は終戦後から。伊勢まで足を運ばなくとも遥拝できるため参拝者も多く、縁結びの神社として名高い。

【主なご利益】縁結び、家内安全、学業成就、商売繁盛、厄除開運など

【特色など】JR飯田橋駅から徒歩約5分

【所在地】東京都千代田区富士見

❻ Hikawa Jinja (Saitama)
Revered from Olden Times for Finding a Marriage Partner

According to shrine records, the shrine was established more than 2,400 years ago and was visited by Yamato Takeru (see page 117) when he came to pacify the eastern provinces. The enshrined deities are the husband and wife pair Susannoo and Inadahime (see page 73), as well as their descendant Onamuchi (see page 75). Onamuchi is, in fact, Okuninushi, the principal god enshrined at Izumo Oyahsiro. From the most ancient times until the present, Hikawa has been known as a shrine that helps find marriage partners and create family happiness.

- **Object of Prayers**: finding marriage partners, childrearing, family happiness, business prosperity, crop protection, and others.

- **Features**: The head shrine of some 280 Hikawa Shrines in Tokyo and Saitama and Kanagawa prefectures.

- **Location**: Takahana-cho, Omiya-ku, Saitama city, Saitama prefecture.

□社記 shrine chronicle
□古来 since olden times
□縁結び bringing people together
□家庭円満 family harmony
□子授け granting of children

❼ Tokyo Dai-jingu (Tokyo)
The Grand Shrine that Began Shinto Weddings

This shrine was established in 1880 with the approval of Emperor Meiji as a venue for offering prayers to Ise Jingu from a distant location. The principal enshrined deities are Amaterasu and Toyouke, with the addition of the Three Gods of Creation (see page 49) and Yamatohime (see page 117). The name became Hibiya Dai-jingu and then Iidabashi Dai-jingu, and then after World War II it assumed its present name. Since it was possible to pay one's respects to Ise Shrine without making the long trip there, the shrine became quite popular and was affectionally called "Oise-sama." It is particularly noted for finding marriage partners.

- **Object of Prayers**: finding marriage partners, family safety, academic success, business prosperity, warding off evil and attracting good fortune, and others.

- **Features**: A 5-minute walk from JR Iidabashi station.

- **Location**: Fujimi, Chiyoda-ku, Tokyo.

□裁可 permission
□遥拝殿 distant shrine
□遥拝する worshipping from afar
□名高い famous

75

❽ 神田神社（東京）

アニメとのコラボもありの江戸総鎮守

日本三大祭の一つの「神田祭」で有名な神社で、通称は「神田明神」。1300年の歴史があるとされ、**江戸時代**には江戸の総鎮守として崇敬された。祭神は、大己貴命（74ページ）と少彦名命（80ページ）の二神および平将門命（148ページ）。都心のオフィス街108町会の総氏神だ。

【主なご利益】縁結び、仕事運、勝運、商売繁盛、健康祈願など

【特色など】アニメ「ラブライブ！」とのコラボレーションで若い参拝者が増加

【所在地】東京都千代田区外神田

❾ 湯島天満宮（東京）

勝負と受験の運気を上げるパワースポット

創建は458年とされ、**当初は**天之手力雄命（62ページ）を祭神としていた。のちに菅原道真（146ページ）も祀られるようになり、江戸時代には徳川将軍家が「学問の神」として尊崇したため、江戸の教育の中心地となった。昔から、二祭神の神徳（力・知恵）にあずかろうという参拝者が多い都心のパワースポットとされてきた。

【主なご利益】勝運、くじ運、学問上達、受験合格など

【特色など】JR御徒町駅から徒歩約8分

【所在地】東京都文京区湯島

❽ Kanda Jinja (Tokyo)

Guardian of the Business District

The Kanda Shrine, also known as Kanda Myojin, is famous for the Kanda Matsuri (Kanda Festival), one of three great Japanese festivals. In the Edo period the shrine was revered as the protector of the city of Edo. It enshrines the deities Onamuchi (see page 75) and Sukunahikona (see page 81), as well as the deified Taira no Masakado (page 149). Kanda Shrine is the guardian shrine for a business district consisting of 108 neighborhood associations.

◆ **Object of Prayers**: finding marriage partners, luck in work, luck in competition, business prosperity, good health, and others.

◆ **Features**: Following the collaborative animation *Rabu Raibu!*, the number of younger visitors to the shrine has increased.

◆ **Location**: Soto-Kanda, Chiyoda-ku, Tokyo.

☐ 通称 commonly known as
☐ 江戸時代 Edo period (1603–1867)

❾ Yushima Tenmangu (Tokyo)

A Power Spot for Increasing One's Fighting Spirit and Exam Success

Founded in 458, Yushima Tenmangu at first enshrined the powerful god Amenotajikarao (see page 63). Later Sugawara no Michizane (see page 147) was added, and since Michizane was venerated as the God of Learning by the Edo shogunate, the area became a center for learning in Edo. It has long been a power spot for visitors hoping to partake of the two virtues of the enshrined gods—physical strength and intelligence.

◆ **Object of Prayers**: luck in competition, luck in lotteries, academic improvement, success in exams, and others.

◆ **Features**: Eight minutes on foot from JR Okachimachi station.

◆ **Location**: Yushima, Bunkyo-ku, Tokyo.

☐ 当初は originally
☐ 神徳 divine attributes

76

❿明治神宮（東京）

日本一の参拝者数を誇る「初詣」

　明治天皇（154ページ）と昭憲皇太后を祀る神社で、創建は1920年。戦時中の空襲で主要建物は焼失したが、1958年に復興造営された。社殿を包む「常磐の森」は、創建時に献木植栽された約10万本の樹木が成長した人工林で、都心の緑のオアシスだ。中心部は内苑と呼ばれ、その外側（外苑）には国立競技場などの諸施設がある。

　【主なご利益】縁結び、家庭円満、商売繁盛など

　【特色など】社殿前の「夫婦楠」は御神木とされる

　【所在地】東京都渋谷区代々木神園町

　【初詣】明治神宮の初詣は12月31日〜1月4日の間で、開門・閉門時間が公開される。参拝者は320万前後と推定され、全国の神社・寺院の中でトップの地位を続けている

　表参道のJR原宿駅は都内最古の木造駅だったが、2020年3月の新駅舎開業に伴い、解体された

明治神宮　初詣

Meiji Jingu: First Visit of the New Year

⑩ Meiji Jingu (Tokyo)
Boosts the Greatest Number of New Year's Visitors

The construction of Meiji Shrine, which is dedicated to the deified spirits of Emperor Meiji (see page 155) and his wife Empress Dowager Shoken, was completed in 1920. The main buildings were lost to fire during World War II but rebuilt in 1958. The forest planted at the time of construction, the Tokiwa no Mori, consists of 100,000 mature trees, and is a virtual oasis in the city center. The core area is called the Naien, and the surrounding area the Gaien, which contains the National Stadium and other facilities.

◆ **Object of Prayers**: finding marriage partners, family happiness, business prosperity, and others.

◆ **Features**: The tree in front of the main hall is called the Husband-Wife Camphor and is considered sacred.

◆ **Location**: Kamizono-cho, Yoyogi, Shibuya-ku, Tokyo.

◆ **First Visit of the New Year**: The first visit of the New Year to Meiji Shrine takes place between December 31 and January 4. The hours when the gates are open and closed to the public are announced beforehand. It is estimated that the shrine attracts something like 3,200,000 visitors, which continues to be the top number for shrines and temples nationwide.
It is accessible from Omotesando's JR Harajuku station, which was the oldest station constructed of wood in the city until dismantlement in March 2020.

☐ 戦時中　wartime
☐ 空襲　air raid
☐ 焼失した　be lost to fire
☐ 復興造営された　be reconstructed and rebuilt
☐ 献木植栽された　be donated and planted
☐ 内苑　inner garden
☐ 外苑　outer garden
☐ 国立競技場　National Stadium
☐ 諸施設　other facilities

⓫水天宮（東京）

77

創成神が祭神の「子授け・安産」の神社

東京の水天宮は元来、九州の久留米藩主の有馬家が屋敷内に造営したもので、参勤交代で江戸に藩主が住むようになったため、1818年に国元から神様を分霊して江戸上屋敷内に祀ったのが始まり。祭神は神々の祖先神・天御中主大神（48ページ）で、子授けや安産に神徳をあらわすと江戸庶民が崇敬したため、有馬家が参拝を許した。

【主なご利益】子授け、安産、水難除けなど

【特色など】平家ゆかりの安徳天皇、建礼門院、二位の尼も祭神として祀る

【所在地】東京都中央区日本橋蛎殻町

⓬鶴岡八幡宮（神奈川）

源 頼朝ゆかりの古都・鎌倉の中心的施設

鎌倉幕府を樹立した源 頼朝が、源氏の氏神として京都の石清水八幡宮を勧請して祀ったのが始まりで、現在地に創建されたのは1191年。以来、関東の総鎮守として江戸幕府も崇敬した。祭神は応神天皇、比売神、神功皇后の三神。本殿と若宮は、国の重要文化財に指定されている。境内社の白旗神社は、頼朝と三代将軍・実朝を祀る。

【主なご利益】勝運、出世運、縁結び、安産など

【特色など】参道は「若宮大路」と呼ばれ、鎌倉市街を南北に貫いている

【所在地】神奈川県鎌倉市雪ノ下

⓫ Suitengu (Tokyo)

Where a Creator God Can Be Petitioned for Pregnancy and Safe Childbirth

The Suitengu shrine in Tokyo was originally located in the precincts of the Kurume domain of the Arima clan in Kyushu. In 1818, as part of the system of alternate attendance (*sankin kotai*), which required feudal lords to live in Edo, the enshrined spirit of the deities in Kurume was split up and transferred to the branch shrine in Edo. The enshrined gods included deified ancestors and the creator god Amenominakanushi (see page 49). Since the townspeople of Edo revered the god-given blessings of the conception of life and safe childbirth, the Arima clan permitted the general public to worship at the shrine.

- ◆ **Object of Prayers**: pregnancy, safe childbirth, prevention of maritime accidents, and others.
- ◆ **Features**: Enshrined deities also include Emperor Antoku, Taira no Tokiko, and Taira no Tokuko, all with Taira connections.
- ◆ **Location**: Nihonbashi-Kakigara-cho, Chuo-ku, Tokyo.

□元来　originally
□参勤交代で　as part of the system of alternate attendance
□藩主　feudal lord
□国元から　from origin
□分霊した　enshrined from the main shrine
□水難　water disaster

⓬ Tsurugaoka Hachimangu (Kanagawa)

The Most Important Shrine in the Old Capital of Kamakura Established by Minamoto no Yoritomo

When establishing Hachimangu in Tsurugaoka, Yoritomo created a branch of the original clan temple in Iwashimizu, Kyoto, and had its deities moved to Kamakura. Tsurugaoka Hachimangu was built in is present location in 1191. Since then it has been considered the guardian deity for the entire Kanto region, and was revered by the Edo shogunate. The enshrined gods are Emperor Ojin, Hime no Kami, and Empress Jingu. The Honden and Wakamiya buildings are national treasures. Within the larger compound is the Shirahata shrine, which enshrines Yoritomo and the 3rd Minamoto shogun, Sanetomo.

- ◆ **Object of Prayers**: luck in competition, success in promotion, luck in finding a marriage partner, safe childbirth, and others.
- ◆ **Features**: The approach to the shrine, the Wakamiya Oji, extends all the way to the ocean, traversing the city from north to south.
- ◆ **Location**: Yukinoshita, Kamakura city, Kanagawa prefecture.

□樹立する　establish
□氏神　clan deity
□若宮　a Shinto shrine dedicated to the deity child of the main shrine deity
□国の重要文化財　national important cultural properties

78

⑬秋葉山本宮秋葉神社（静岡）

サブカルチャーの聖地アキバはこの社名にちなむ

　浜松の秋葉山の山頂付近にある神社で、709年の創建とされる。江戸時代まで秋葉大権現社と秋葉寺が同じ境内にあり、**明治**の**神仏分離令**で神社だけが残って「秋葉神社」と改称。祭神は、火之迦具土大神とされた。この神はイザナミが産んだ子の一人で(52ページ)、火の神であることから「**火災鎮護の神**」とされてきた。

【**主なご利益**】火災消除、商売繁盛、作業安全、交通安全、安産など

【**特色など**】末社は400社以上あるとされ、東京の秋葉神社（台東区）は「あきば」と読む

【**所在地**】浜松市天竜区春野町

⑭富士山本宮浅間大社（静岡）

霊峰・富士を女神として祀る浅間神社の総本宮

　古代人は、しばしば大噴火を起こす富士山を怖れた。山霊を鎮めるために浅間大神を祀ったのが神社の起源とされる。この**大神**は木花之佐久夜毘売命とされ、夫の瓊々杵尊と父の大山祇神の二神も祭神として祀る(98ページ)。富士山信仰の広まりと共に全国に造営された1300余りの浅間神社の総本宮だ。なお、山頂には**奥宮**がある。

【**主なご利益**】火難消除、安産、家庭円満、航海・産業守護など

【**特色など**】2013年6月、「富士山—信仰の対象と芸術の源泉」として世界文化遺産に登録

【**所在地**】静岡県富士宮市宮町

⓭ Akihasan Hongu Akiha Jinja (Shizuoka)

The Subculture Mecca Akihabara Takes Its Name from This Shrine

Located on the summit of Mount Akiha in Hamamatsu, the shrine was constructed in 709. Until the Edo period the Akiha Dai-gongensha shrine and Akihadera temple occupied the same precinct, but with the Meiji law separating Buddhism and Shinto, only the shrine remains, renamed the Akiha Jinja. Its god became Hinokagutsuchi. He was one of the children of Izanami (see page 53). Being the God of Fire, he has been considered a guardian god against disaster by fire.

◆ **Object of Prayers**: extinguishing fires, business prosperity, safety in working, safe childbirth, and others.

◆ **Features**: There are more than 400 branch temples nationwide. The one in Tokyo (Taito-ku) is called "Akiba Jinja."

◆ **Location**: Haruno-cho, Tenryu-ku, Hamamatsu, Shizuoka prefecture.

☐ 明治 Meiji period (1868–1912)

☐ 神仏分離令 Shinto and Buddhism Separation Order

☐ 改称 rename

☐ 火災鎮護 fire protection

☐ 火災消除 fire extinguishing

⓮ Fujisan Hongu Sengen Taisha (Shizuoka)

Head Asama Shrine Dedicated to the Goddess of Mount Fuji and Its Summit

The ancients feared frequently erupting Mount Fuji. Sengen Shrine was established to pacify the spirit of the mountain, as well as Konohanasakuya and her father Oyamazumi, which are also gods of the mountain (see page 99). As the religious following of Mount Fuji spread around the country, so did the number of more than 1,300 Sengen (Asama) shrines, of which Fujisan Hongu Sengen Taisha is the head organization. On the summit there is a small shrine called an *okumiya*.

◆ **Object of Prayers**: avoidance of fire, easy birth, happy families, safe navigation, business preservation, and others.

◆ **Features**: In June 2013 UNESCO designated Mount Fuji as a sacred place and source of artistic inspiration.

◆ **Location**: Miya-cho, Fujinomiya, Shizuoka prefecture.

☐ 噴火を起こす erupt

☐ 山霊 spirit of the mountain

☐ 大神 great deity

☐ 奥宮 a shrine with the same deity and located further back than the main shrine

79

⑮ 諏訪大社（長野）

諏訪湖 周 辺に４か所の境内地をもつ古社

国内最古の神社の一つとされ、『古事記』や『日本書紀』にも登場する。祭神は、建御名 方 神（84ページ）と八坂刀売神の夫婦神。『古事記』ではオオクニヌシの息子の建御名 方 神が、天神に追われてこの地で降伏したとされるが、地元では先住の神々を降伏させた武勇の神としてきた。今は、生活の 源 を守る神と崇められている。

【主 なご利益】産業守護、勝運、開運、縁結び、子授けなど

【特色など】南に「上社前宮」「上社本宮」、北に「下社春宮」「下社秋宮」の４社がある

【所在地】長野県諏訪市

【御柱祭】７年目ごとにおこなわれる大祭。４つの社殿の四隅に山から伐り出した樹齢200年ほどの巨木を立てる神事で、**御柱が坂を下る「木落し」**や川を曳き渡る「川越し」は度胸試しとしても有名である。諏訪大社の分社は、１万社以上あるとされる

諏訪大社　御柱 祭「木落し」
Onbashira Festival, Suwa Taisha

⓯ Suwa Taisha (Nagano)
An Ancient Shrine with Four Compounds near Lake Suwa

Considered one of the oldest shrines in Japan, Suwa Taisha is mentioned in the *Kojiki* and *Nihon Shoki*. The enshrined deities are the husband and wife Takeminakata (see page 85) and Yasakatome. According to the *Kojiki*, Takeminakata (the son of Okuninushi) was forced by the heavenly gods to descend to this area, where he was considered a heroic god for defeating the local earthly gods. Now he is worshipped as the guardian god of daily life.

- **Object of Prayers**: guardian of business, lucky in competition, improved fortune, marriage partners, pregnancy, and others.

- **Features**: There are four shrines in the Suwa Taisha complex: Kamisha Maemiya and Kamisha Honmiya in the south, and Shimosha Harumiya and Shimosha Akimiya in the north.

- **Location**: Suwa city, Nagano prefecture.

- **Onbashira Festival**: This grand religious festival is held every seven years. It consists of four huge wooden pillars of about 200 years in age being cut down from the mountains and raised in the four corners of four shrine buildings. Getting trees down the mountain and transporting them across a river is considered a test of courage. There are more than 10,000 branches of Suwa Taisha throughout the country.

□源 source
□四隅 four corners
□伐り出した felled
□御柱が坂を下る dropping of the tree down the hill
□川を曳き渡る pulling across the river
□度胸試し test of courage

西日本
にし　に　ほん
West Japan

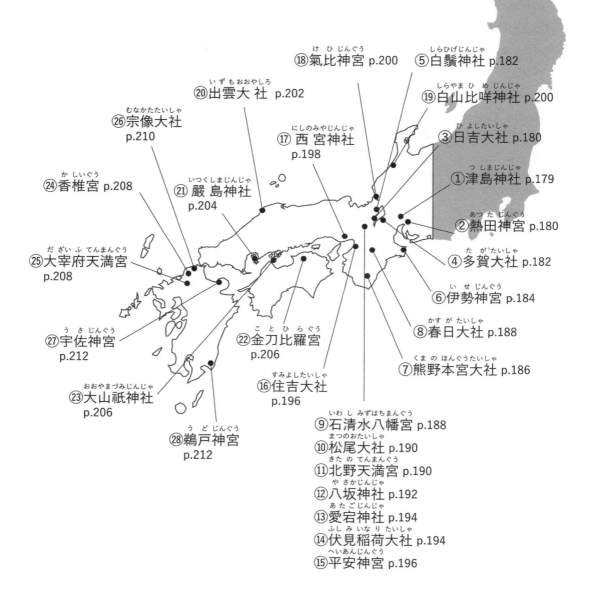

⑱氣比神宮 p.200
け　ひ　じんぐう

⑤白鬚神社 p.182
しらひげじんじゃ

⑳出雲大社 p.202
いず　も　おおやしろ

⑲白山比咩神社 p.200
しらやま　ひ　め　じんじゃ

㉖宗像大社 p.210
むなかたたいしゃ

⑰西宮神社 p.198
にしのみやじんじゃ

③日吉大社 p.180
ひ　よしたいしゃ

①津島神社 p.179
つ　しまじんじゃ

㉔香椎宮 p.208
か　しいぐう

㉑嚴島神社 p.204
いつくしまじんじゃ

②熱田神宮 p.180
あつ　た　じんぐう

④多賀大社 p.182
た　が　たいしゃ

㉕大宰府天満宮 p.208
だ　ざい　ふ　てんまんぐう

⑥伊勢神宮 p.184
い　せ　じんぐう

㉗宇佐神宮 p.212
う　さ　じんぐう

㉒金刀比羅宮 p.206
こと　ひ　らぐう

⑧春日大社 p.188
かす　が　たいしゃ

⑦熊野本宮大社 p.186
くま　の　ほんぐうたいしゃ

㉓大山祇神社 p.206
おおやまづみじんじゃ

⑯住吉大社 p.196
すみよしたいしゃ

㉘鵜戸神宮 p.212
う　ど　じんぐう

⑨石清水八幡宮 p.188
いわ　し　みずはちまんぐう

⑩松尾大社 p.190
まつのおたいしゃ

⑪北野天満宮 p.190
きた　の　てんまんぐう

⑫八坂神社 p.192
や　さかじんじゃ

⑬愛宕神社 p.194
あ　た　ごじんじゃ

⑭伏見稲荷大社 p.194
ふし　み　いな　り　たいしゃ

⑮平安神宮 p.196
へいあんじんぐう

① 津島神社（愛知）

80

戦国大名も崇敬したスサノオを主祭神とする天王社

1500年近い歴史をもつと伝えられ、古くは牛頭天王（神仏習合の神）信仰の中心社とされた。主祭神は建速須佐之男命（60ページ）で、大穴牟遅命（74ページ）も祭神として祀られている。織田信長を氏神とし、豊臣家や徳川家も建物を寄進するなど、戦国大名にも崇敬された。江戸時代には、「津島詣」が大流行した。

【主なご利益】除厄、授福など

【特色など】全国に約3000ある「津島神社」「天王社」の総本社。日本三大川祭りの一つの「尾張津島天王祭」は世界無形文化遺産に登録

【所在地】愛知県津島市神明町

① Tsushima Jinja (Aichi)

A Tennosha Shrine Dedicated to Susanoo and Revered by Feudal Lords of the Warring States Period

With a history stretching back nearly 1,500 years, of old it was the central shrine of the religious sect devoted to the Shinto-Buddhist syncretic god Gozu Tenno. Its chief enshrined deity was Takehaya Susanoo (see page 61), joined by Onamuchi (see page 75). Oda Nobunaga was its tutelary spirit, and the Toyotomi and Tokugawa families both contributed to its repair and construction, showing the reverence held by the Warring States lords for the shrine. In the Edo period pilgrimages to Tsushima shrine enjoyed a great fad.

◆ **Object of Prayers**: avoiding evil, attracting good fortune, and others.

◆ **Features**: The head temple of some 3,000 Tsushima Jinja and Tennosha shrines throughout the country. The Owari Tsushima Tenno Matsuri, one of the three greatest river festivals in Japan, has been designated an Intangible Cultural Heritage.

◆ **Location**: Shinmei-cho, Tsushima city, Aichi prefecture.

□寄進する　contribute
□授福　bestowal of blessings

81

② 熱田神宮（愛知）

皇室の祖神アマテラスゆかりの神剣を祀る

主祭神の熱田大神は、三種の神器の一つ「草薙神剣」を御霊代として依る天照大神である。この神剣はヤマトタケルに受け継がれ、その死後に妻が熱田の地に祀ったのが由来とされる（118ページ）。また、神剣にゆかりが深い五神を相殿神として祀る。伊勢神宮（184ページ）に次ぐ格式の高い大社とされてきた。

【主なご利益】縁結び、出世運、家内安全、商売繁盛など

【特色など】本宮のほか別宮・摂社・末社など40数社がある

【所在地】名古屋市熱田区神宮

③ 日吉大社（滋賀）

東西二つの本宮がある比叡山麓の古社

『古事記』では、日枝の山（比叡山）にいる大山咋神の存在を記している。この神はスサノオ（60ページ）の孫ともされ、酒造りの神として古くから崇敬されてきた。主祭神として、東本宮で祀られている。一方、西本宮の主祭神は大己貴神（74ページ）。また、大社は比叡山延暦寺の守護神「山王権現」とも呼ばれる。

【主なご利益】縁結び、厄除け、方除けなど

【特色など】全国に3800余りある「日吉神社」「日枝神社」「山王神社」の総本宮

【所在地】滋賀県大津市坂本

② **Atsuta Jingu (Aichi)**

Enshrines the Sacred Sword Handed down from Amaterasu, Ancestor of the Imperial Family

The chief enshrined object at Atsuta Jingu is the sacred sword Kusanagi, which is one of the three regalia of the imperial house and a spiritual substitute for Amaterasu. This sword was passed down to Yamato Takeru, and after his death his wife enshrined it in the Atsuta region (see page 119). Further, the Five Great Gods of Atsuta, with deep connections to the sacred sword, are enshrined in a separate structure. Atsuta Jingu has the next highest rank as a shrine after Ise Jingu (see page 185).

- **Object of Prayers**: finding marriage partners, success in life, household safety, business prosperity, and others.

- **Features**: Aside from the main hall, the precinct includes some forty buildings, such as the *betsugu*, *sessha*, and *massha*.

- **Location**: Jingu, Atsuta-ku, Nagoya city, Aichi prefecture.

☐ 御霊代 spiritual surrogate

☐ 相殿神 associated deity/ deities enshrined alongside the main deity.

③ **Hiyoshi Taisha (Shiga)**

An Ancient Shrine with Two Main Halls in East and West

The *Kojiki* records the existence of the god Oyamakui residing in Mount Hie. He is said to be the grandson of Susanoo (see page 61), and has long been revered as the god of sake brewing. He is enshrined as the chief god in the East Main Hall. The god of the West Main Hall is Onamuchi (see page 75). Both deities were made guardian gods of Enryakuji temple on Mount Hiei under the name Sanno Gongen.

- **Object of Prayers**: finding a marriage partner, avoiding evil, avoiding bad directions, and others.

- **Features**: The head shrine of more than 3,800 Hiyoshi Jinja, Hie Jinja, and Sanno Jinja shrines throughout the country.

- **Location**: Sakamoto, Otsu city, Shiga prefecture.

☐ 方除け ritual practice to ward off evil spirits and bring good fortune

82

④ 多賀大社(滋賀)

イザナギとイザナミを祀る「お多賀さん」

　日本神話の「国生み、神生み」で知られる伊邪那岐大神・伊邪那美大神の夫婦神(50ページ)を祀るこの神社は、古くから「お多賀さん」と呼ばれて崇敬されてきた。鎌倉時代から江戸時代にかけては、武家や庶民にも信仰が広まり、大社の分祀社は全国に239社を数える。豊臣秀吉が母親の病気平癒を祈ったことでも知られる。

【主なご利益】縁結び、延命長寿など

【特色など】豊臣秀吉が寄進したとされる奥書院庭園は国指定名勝

【所在地】滋賀県多賀町多賀

⑤ 白鬚神社(滋賀)

湖中に大鳥居がある近江最古の大社

　琵琶湖の北西に位置する神社の創建は、約2000年前と伝わる。祭神は猿田彦命で、ニニギの「天孫降臨」(94ページ)のときに道案内をした国神だ。そのため「導き・道開きの神」として各地で崇敬され、現代にも全国に約300の分霊社が存在している。なお、「ひげ」の漢字を「髭」「髯」と表記する分社もある。

【主なご利益】延命長寿、交通安全、縁結び、子授けなど

【特色など】琵琶湖に浮かぶ大鳥居は撮影スポットとして人気が高い

【所在地】滋賀県高島市鵜川

④ **Taga Taisha (Shiga)**
Enshrining Izanagi and Izanami, Familiarly Known O-Tagasan

Taga Taisha enshrines the husband and wife deities Izanagi and Izanami, who gave birth to the islands and gods of Japan (see page 51). Its followers expanded from the Kamakura period into the Edo period among both common people and the samurai class, until it reached 239 branches nationwide. Notably, the great warrior and political leader Toyotomi Hideyoshi visited the shrine to pray for his ailing mother.

- **Object of Prayers**: finding a marriage partner, enjoying a long and fruitful life, and others.

- **Features**: The Oku Shoin garden, donated by Toyotomi Hideyoshi, has been designated a Place of Scenic Beauty by the Japanese government.

- **Location**: Taga, Taga-cho, Shiga prefecture.

□ 分祀社 branch shrine or detached shrine

□ 国指定名勝 Place of Scenic Beauty designated by the national government

⑤ **Shirahige Jinja (Shiga)**
The Oldest Shrine in Omi with a *Torii* Gate Standing in Lake Biwa

Shirahige Jinja, located in the north-west part of Lake Biwa, is said to have been founded about 2,000 years ago. The enshrined god is Sarutahiko, an earthly god who acted as a guide when Ninigi descended to earth (see page 95). Consequently, Sarutahiko is widely venerated as a guide and pathfinder, and even today there are some 300 branch shrines around the country. For the word *hige* (鬚) in the name of the shrine, some shrines use 髭 or 髯.

- **Object of Prayers**: a long and fruitful life, traffic safety, finding a marriage partner, pregnancy, and others.

- **Features**: The *torii* standing in the water of Lake Biwa is a favorite spot for photographers.

- **Location**: Ukawa, Takashima city, Shiga prefecture.

□ 導き・道開きの神 deity of guidance and path opening

□ 分霊社 branch shrine or detached shrine dedicated to a portion of the main deity's spirit

83

⑥伊勢神宮（三重）

20年ごとに建替えられる古代建築様式の神殿

2000年以上の歴史をもつ、この神社の正式名称は「神宮」。天皇家の祖神・天照大御神（60ページ）を祀る内宮（皇大神宮）、豊受大御神を祀る外宮（豊受大神宮）は、20年ごとに一新される。豊受大御神は食物の神でもあり、外宮では毎日朝夕、天照大御神の食事を作って供える「大御饌祭」がおこなわれている。

【主なご利益】（外宮）衣食住、商売繁盛など

【特色など】神宮は伊勢市周辺の125宮社の総称。内宮では三種の神器の一つ「八咫鏡」（42ページ）を御神体として祀る

【所在地】三重県伊勢市

【式年遷宮】内宮と外宮にはそれぞれ東西に同じ広さの敷地があり、20年に一度、宮地を改め社殿や神宝を一新する。1300年間にわたって続くとされる神宮最大の神事で、2013年（第62回）は8年もの準備期間を要した

伊勢神宮　内宮

Ise Jingu: The Interior Shrine

⑥ Ise Jingu (Mie)
Rebuilt Every Twenty Years in the Original Style

The official name of Ise Jingu, with a history of over 2,000 years, is simply "Jingu." The Interior Shrine (Naiku or Kotai Jingu) enshrines the divine ancestor of the imperial family, Amaterasu (see page 61), and the Outer Shrine (Geku or Toyouke Dai-jingu) enshrines the deity Toyouke, both structures being rebuilt every twenty years. Toyouke is the god of agriculture, and every morning in the Outer Shrine food is prepared for Amaterasu in a special ceremony called Omikesai.

◆ **Object of Prayers**: (Outer Shrine) food, clothing, and shelter, business prosperity, and others.

◆ **Features**: "Jingu" refers in general to the 125 shrines in Ise city and the surrounding area. The Inner Shrine enshrines the Yata no Kagami (see page 43), a sacred mirror that is part of the imperial regalia and a deified object of worship.

◆ **Location**: Ise city, Mie prefecture.

◆ **Rebuilding the Shrine [Shikinen Sengu]**: The buildings and precious objects of the Interior and Outer Shrines, which occupy the same amount of space from east to west, are rebuilt and renewed every 20 years. This momentous event has been ongoing for 1,300 years; the last rebuilding (the 62th) took 8 years to complete in 2013.

□ 正式名称 official designation

□ 内宮 Naiku (Inner Shrine)

□ 外宮 Geku (Outer Shrine)

□ 20年ごとに一新される undergo a complete rebuilding every 20 years

□ 大御饌祭 Omike Festival (Great Offering Ceremony)

□ 式年遷宮 Shikinen Sengu (ceremonial relocation of the shrines)

□ 宮地 shrine grounds

□ 神宝 sacred objects and regalia

84

⑦ 熊野本宮大社(和歌山)

世界遺産・熊野古道に位置する神仏習合の聖地

「神武東征」神話(108ページ)に登場する熊野は、3600峰と呼ばれる山々が連なる深山幽谷の地。山間を蛇行して太平洋に至る熊野川の中枢にあるのが、この大社だ。主祭神は樹木の支配神・家都美子大神で、素戔嗚尊(60ページ)と同一視される。他に12柱の神々を祀るが、いずれも仏・菩薩を仮の姿とする神仏習合の権現神である。

【主なご利益】厄除け、水難除け、開運、縁結びなど

【特色など】熊野三山(本宮大社・速玉大社・那智大社)の中心。全国に約5000社ある熊野神社の総本宮

【所在地】和歌山県田辺市本宮町

【那智大滝】高さ133m、落ち口の幅13m、滝つぼの深さ約10mの大滝は、「日本三名瀑」に数えられ、国指定名勝。熊野三山「熊野那智大社」の別宮「飛瀧神社」の御神体である。2004年、「紀伊山地の霊場と参詣道」が世界文化遺産に登録

那智大滝

Nachi Falls

⑦ Kumano Hongu Taisha (Wakayama)

Designated a World Heritage Site as Part of the Sacred Sites and Pilgrimage Routes in the Kii Mountain Range

The Kumano region, with its self-proclaimed series of 3,600 steep peaks and deep valleys, appears in the myth of the East Expedition of Emperor Jinmu (see page 109). Kumano Hongu Taisha lies at the heart of this region, and the Kumano river wanders through its mountains until it reaches the Pacific Ocean. The chief enshrined god is the protector of trees, Ketsumiko, who is considered equivalent to Susanoo (see page 61). There are 12 other enshrined gods, but they are all so-called *gongen* gods—that is, buddhas or bodhisattvas that have manifested themselves as Japanese *kami* in order to better teach Buddhism to the Japanese people.

- **Object of Prayers**: avoid evil, avoid maritime accidents, gain good fortune, find a marriage partner, and others.

- **Features**: Kumano Hongu Taisha is the centerpiece of the Kumano Sanzan complex of shrines, which includes Hongu Taisha, Hayatama Taisha, and Nachi Taisha. It is the head shrine of 5,000 Kumano Jinja nationwide.

- **Location**: Hongu-cho, Tanabe city, Wakayama prefecture.

- **Nachi Falls**: With a drop of 133 meters, a width of 13 meters at the head, and a basin with a width of 10 meters, it is counted as one of the three great Japanese waterfalls. It has been designated a Place of Scenic Beauty by the Japanese government. The Falls itself is the object of worship of the subsidiary shrine Hiro Jinja of Kumano Sanzan's Nachi Taisha. In 2004 it was designated a World Heritage site as part of the Sacred Sites and Pilgrimage Routes in the Kii Mountain Range.

□ 峰 peak or summit

□ 深山幽谷の地 a secluded area deep in the mountains

□ 蛇行する meander or wind through

□ ～の中枢にある lie at the heart of

□ ～と同一視される be equated with or considered identical to

□ 権現神 syncretic deities combining Shinto and Buddhist elements

□ 日本三名瀑 Three Great Waterfalls of Japan

85

⑧ 春日大社(奈良)

鹿を神使とする藤原氏の氏神を祀る神社

奈良・平城京が都となった8世紀、権勢を誇った藤原氏が春日の御蓋山に氏神の4神を祀る社殿を造営したのが始まりと伝わる。この神々は、武甕槌命(84ページ)、経津主命(162ページ)、天児屋根命(62ページ)・比売神の夫婦神。武甕槌命が鹿島(茨城)から白鹿に乗ってきたとの伝説から、鹿を神使として保護している。

【主なご利益】開運、縁結び、夫婦円満など

【特色など】国宝殿は、国宝・重要文化財1300点以上を所蔵。1998年登録の世界文化遺産「古都奈良の文化財」に、大社と春日山原始林が含まれる

【所在地】奈良県奈良市春日野町

⑨ 石清水八幡宮(京都)

伊勢神宮と共に宗廟とされてきた京の守護社

京都盆地の南西に位置する男山の山上にあり、860年の創建とされる。京都の裏鬼門の守護社として天皇家をはじめ貴族や武家が崇敬してきた。主祭神は八幡大神で、本源は宇佐神宮(212ページ)にある。源氏の氏神とされ、源頼朝の勧請で鎌倉に鶴岡八幡宮(172ページ)が築造された。日本三大八幡宮の一社。

【主なご利益】勝運、厄除け、安産など

【特色など】2016年、本殿をはじめとする10の建造物などが国宝に指定された

【所在地】京都府八幡市八幡高坊

⑧ **Kasuga Taisha (Nara)**
Protecting Deer as Messengers of the Gods

Kasuga Taisha had its beginnings in the 8th century when Nara (i.e., Heijo) became the capital and the powerful Fujiwara family built a shrine dedicated to four tutelary gods on Mount Mikasa in Kasuga. These four gods were Takemikazuchi (see page 85), Futsunushi (see page 163), Amenokoyane (see page 63) and his wife Hime. From the legend that Takemikazuchi came from Kashima ("Deer Island") in Ibaraki prefecture riding a white deer has led to the present-day protection of deer at Kasuga.

- ◆ **Object of Prayers**: good fortune, finding a marriage partner, good marital relations, and others.

- ◆ **Features**: Within the shrine itself (a national treasure) are housed over 1,300 national treasures and important cultural properties. In 1998 the shrine and the nearby Kasugayama Primeval Forest were registered as a UNESCO World Heritage Site as part of the Historic Monuments of Ancient Nara.

- ◆ **Location**: Kasugano-cho, Nara city, Nara prefecture.

- □ 白鹿 sacred white deer
- □ 神使 divine messenger
- □ 国宝殿 Hall of National Treasures
- □ 国宝 designated national treasure
- □ 重要文化財 designated important cultural property
- □ 所蔵する house
- □ 春日山原始林 Kasugayama Primeval Forest

⑨ **Iwashimizu Hachimangu (Kyoto)**
Together with Ise Jingu, One of Two Imperial Mausoleums and a Kyoto Guardian Shrine

Said to have been constructed in 860, the shrine is situated in the northwest of the Kyoto basin on Mount Otokoyama. It was meant to protect the city from the unlucky southwestern direction, and was highly revered by the aristocratic and samurai classes, not to mention the imperial family. The chief enshrined deity is Hachiman, whose origin is the deity Hachiman in Usa (see page 213). He is said to be the tutelary god of the Genji clan, whose spirit was re-enshrined at Tsurugaoka Hachimangu when it was built in Kamakura (see page 173). It is one of the three greatest Hachimangu shrines in the country.

- ◆ **Object of Prayers**: lucky in competition, avoiding evil, safe childbirth, and others.

- ◆ **Features**: In 2016 the main hall and ten other buildings were designated national treasures.

- ◆ **Location**: Yawata Takabo, Yawata city, Kyoto.

- □ 宗廟 imperial shrine
- □ 裏鬼門 Ura-Kimon: The southwest direction in traditional Japanese house design (Kasō). It is considered an unlucky direction, similar to the Kimon (鬼門) in the northeast.
- □ 本源 source

86

⑩ 松尾大社（京都）

酒神として崇敬された京都最古の神社

701年、文武天皇の勅命で渡来系氏族の秦氏が創建したとされる。平安京遷都後は王城鎮護社として、東の賀茂神社に対して西の松尾神社と並び称された。祭神は大山咋神（180ページ）と中津島姫命（市杵島姫命、210ページ）で、松尾山を御神体とする。中世以降は「酒神」としても信仰され、現在も酒造家が崇敬する。

【主なご利益】酒業繁栄、健康長寿、開運出世、縁結びなど

【特色など】本殿は室町時代の造営で、国重要文化財。亀を神使とする

【所在地】京都市西京区嵐山宮町

⑪ 北野天満宮（京都）

全国に1万2000社もある天神信仰の総本社

菅原道真（146ページ）の死後、有志によって創建された（947年）。のちに皇室が崇敬するところとなり、国家国民を守護する霊験あらたかな神として「天神信仰」が定着した。京都市民は「天神さん」とか「北野さん」と親しみをこめて呼ぶ。江戸時代には「学芸の神」として崇敬され、全国に分霊された。

【主なご利益】学業成就、子育て、開運、金運など

【特色など】牛を神使とする。神社の牛像の頭をなでると頭が良くなる、病気の部分をなでると病気が治るといったご利益のある「なで牛」が有名

【所在地】京都市上京区馬喰町

⑩ **Matsunoo Taisha (Kyoto)**

Kyoto's Oldest Temple, Enshrining the God of Sake

Matsunoo Taisha was built by the immigrant Hata clan at the behest of Emperor Monmu in 701. After the capital was moved from Nara to Kyoto, the temple became a guardian of the city in the west in contrast to Kamo Shrine in the east. The enshrined gods are Oyamakui (see page 181) and Nakatsushima (Ichikishima, see page 211); Mount Matsunoo is the deified object of worship. After the medieval period the worship of the "god of sake" became more widely practiced, and the god was much revered in the homes of sake brewers.

- ❖ **Object of Prayers**: prosperity of sake brewing, a long and healthy life, good luck and success in life, finding a marriage partner, and others.

- ❖ **Features**: The main hall, constructed in the Muromachi period (1336–1573), has been designated an important cultural property by the Japanese government. It takes the turtle as a messenger from the gods.

- ❖ **Location**: Arashiyama Miya-machi, Nishikyo-ku, Kyoto.

- ☐ 勅命 imperial decree
- ☐ 渡来系氏族 clan of immigrants from the Korean peninsula
- ☐ 遷都 moving the capital
- ☐ 酒神 deity of sake
- ☐ 酒造家 sake brewery
- ☐ 酒業 sake brewing industry
- ☐ 室町時代 Muromachi period (1336-1573)
- ☐ 亀 sacred turtle

⑪ **Kitano Tenmangu (Kyoto)**

The Headquarters of 12,000 Tenjin Shrines Nationwide

After Sugawara no Michizane's death (see page 147), this shrine was erected by his devotees in 947. Later Michizane came to be revered by the imperial family and seen as a miracle-working god who could protect the country and its people. The worship of Michizane, or Tenjin, became established. The people of Kyoto affectionately called him Tenjin-san or Kitano-san. In the Edo period he became revered as the god of learning, and his spirit became deified in shrines throughout the country.

- ❖ **Object of Prayers**: academic achievement, childrearing, good luck, financial good fortune, and others.

- ❖ **Features**: The ox is considered a messenger of the gods. If one rubs the head of the ox statue at the shrine, one will gain a good head. If one rubs the part of a statue where one is ailing, that part will heal. This so-called "rubbing the ox" is widely known.

- ❖ **Location**: Bakuro-cho, Kamigyo-ku, Kyoto.

- ☐ 有志 worshipper
- ☐ 霊験あらたかな known for its miraculous powers
- ☐ 学芸の神 deity of learning and the arts
- ☐ 学業成就 academic success
- ☐ なでる pet
- ☐ なで牛 rubbing statue of a ox

⑫ 八坂神社（京都）

病魔退散を祈る神事が起源となった祇園祭

創建は656年（876年説もある）と伝えられ、古くは牛頭天王（インドの祇園精舎の守護神）を祀っていた。この神は**防疫の神**だったため京都に疫病が流行した869年、**病魔退散の御霊会**がおこなわれた。これが祇園祭の起源である。明治以降、祭神は素戔嗚尊・櫛稲田姫命の夫婦神（72ページ）および八柱御子神の8神とされた。

　【**主なご利益**】厄除け、開運、文芸上達など

　【**特色など**】境内社として、美と芸能と**財福**の「美御前社」、縁結びの「大国主社」、悪縁を切る「刃物社」などがある

　【**所在地**】京都市東山区祇園町

　【**祇園祭**】例年7月1日から1か月にわたって開催され、京都の夏の風物誌となっている。山車が市内を巡る「**山鉾巡行**」は山鉾町が主催し、神社が主催するのは「**神輿渡御**」「**神輿洗**」に代表される神事である

　京都の総本社にならって、全国各地の八坂系神社も「祇園祭」を催行している

祇園 祭
Gion Festival

⑫ Yasaka Jinja (Kyoto)
The Gion Festival Originates in Prayer Rites to Expel Disease

Built in 656 (or 876 according to one theory), from olden times the Yasaka Jinja enshrined Gozu Tenno (a guardian god of the first monastery built for the Buddha in India). Since Gozu Tenno was a god who prevented epidemics, a seance was held to appease him when disease broke out in 869. This proved to be the origin of the Gion Festival. From the Meiji period onward there were eight deities enshrined at the shrine, including Susanoo/Kushinadahime (husband and wife; see page 73) and Yahashira.

- **Object of Prayers**: warding off evil, inviting good fortune, improvement of literary skills, and others.

- **Features**: Within the shrine's precincts are lesser shrines devoted to art, literature, and wealth such as Bigozensha, to finding marriage partners like Okuninushisha, and to cutting ties with evil like Hamono-sha.

- **Location**: Gion-machi, Higashiyama-ku, Kyoto.

- **Gion Festival**: This festival, held every year for one month starting on July 1, is one of the most distinguishing events of the Kyoto summer season. The floats called *dashi* and *yamahoko* that parade the streets are sponsored by the Yamahoko Neighborhood Association, and the parade and ritualistic purification of the miniature shrines called *mikoshi* are sponsored by the shrine.
Following the lead of the head shrine, Yasaka shrines throughout the country hold their own Gion festivals.

□祇園精舎 the first Buddhist monastery in India
□防疫の神 deity of epidemic prevention
□病魔退散 ward off evil spirits and disease
□御霊会 festival to appease the spirits of the dead
□文芸上達 improvement in literary skills and artistic talents
□財福 prosperity, wealth, and good fortune
□悪縁を切る severing ties with bad relationships
□刃物 knives and other sharp objects
□夏の風物誌 summer tradition
□山鉾巡行 parade of floats
□神輿渡御 procession of portable shrines
□神輿洗 purification ritual for portable shrines
□催行する hold

88

⑬ 愛宕神社（京都）

「火廼要慎」のお札で知られる古社

　京都市の標高924mの愛宕山上にあり、創建は8世紀初頭と伝わる。旧称は阿多古神社で、神仏習合の**山岳信仰の聖地**として知られ、全国に約900社を数える愛宕神社の本社である。祭神は本殿と若宮に8神祀られ、その一柱の迦遇槌命（52ページ）は「**防火の神**」として崇敬されてきた。「愛宕さん」とも呼ばれる。

　【主なご利益】火除け、厄除け、縁結びなど
　【特色など】例年7月31日夜から8月1日早朝におこなわれる「千日通夜祭」は
　　　　　1000日分のご利益があるとされる
　【所在地】京都市右京区嵯峨愛宕町

⑭ 伏見稲荷大社（京都）

全国に約3万社とされる稲荷神社の総本宮

　五穀の豊作をつかさどる「**倉稲魂**」を祀ったのが**稲荷神社**で、起源は山の神への信仰ともいわれる。稲作の広まりと共に各地に稲荷信仰が**根付き**、その総本宮としての**稲荷山麓の伏見稲荷**の権威が高まった。創建は711年とされ、942年に朝廷から最高の**神階**である正一位に叙せられた。主祭神は、稲荷大神（4柱の神の総称）。

　【主なご利益】商売繁盛、安産、万病平癒、学業成就など
　【特色など】狐を神使とする。寄進で増え続ける赤い「千本鳥居」が有名
　【所在地】京都市伏見区深草藪之内町

⑬ **Atago Jinja (Kyoto)**
An Old Shrine Famous for Its "Beware of Fire!" Talismans

Situated atop Kyoto's 924-meter Mount Atago, this shrine is said to have been erected at the beginning of the 8th century. Originally the name of the shrine was 阿多古神社, which is homophonous with its present name (愛宕神社), and was considered sacred ground to those who believed the mountain was an incarnation of a Buddha or Japanese god. It is the head shrine of some 900 Atago shrines nationwide. Altogether there are eight gods enshrined in the main hall and the secondary *wakamiya*, of which one, Kagutsuchi, is revered as the god of fire (see page 53). The shrine is affectionately referred to as Atago-san.

- ❖ **Object of Prayers**: avoidance of fire, warding off evil, finding a marriage partner, and others.

- ❖ **Features**: It is said that those who attend the Thousand Day Wake Festival (Sennichi Tsuyasai), held from the night of July 31 to the morning of August 1, will have a thousand days of prayers answered.

- ❖ **Location**: Saga Atago-cho, Ukyo-ku, Kyoto.

☐ 火廼要慎 Fire Hazard
☐ 旧称は Formerly known as
☐ 山岳信仰 mountain worship
☐ 聖地 sacred place
☐ 防火の神 deity of fire prevention

⑭ **Fushimi Inari Taisha (Kyoto)**
The Headquarters of 30,000 Fushimi Inari Shrines Nationwide

Inari shrine is dedicated to Ukanomitama, the god of food and agriculture, and is said to have its beginnings in the worship of Mount Inari. With the spread of rice cultivation, the worship of Inari became established here and there, and the prestige of Inari Grand Shrine at the foot of Mount Inari grew as the head shrine. It is said to have been erected in 711, and in 942 the imperial court awarded it the highest rank for a shrine, *shoichi-i*. The principal enshrined god, Inari Okami, is a composite of four gods.

- ❖ **Object of Prayers**: business prosperity, easy birth, panacea for all illnesses, scholarly achievement, and others.

- ❖ **Features**: The fox is the messenger of the gods. The red "Thousand *Torii*," which continue to grow in number through contributions, is particularly famous.

- ❖ **Location**: Fukakusa Yabunouchi-cho, Fushimi-ku, Kyoto.

☐ 五穀の豊作 bountiful harvest of five grains
☐ つかさどる responsible for
☐ 稲荷神社 Inari shrine
☐ 根付く become established
☐ 稲荷山麓 foot of Mount Inari
☐ 神階 divine rank
☐ 正一位 the highest rank for a shrine
☐ 叙せられる be bestowed

89

⑮ 平安神宮（京都）

遷都1100年を記念して造営された神宮

明治維新で衰退した京都の復興を目的に、1895年に創建された。社殿は平安京遷都当時の大内裏を8分の5の規模で復元したもの。祭神は当初、平安京遷都をおこなった50代桓武天皇とされていたが、1940年に121代孝明天皇が合祀された。例年10月22日に催行される「時代祭」は、京都三大祭の一つである。

【主なご利益】縁結び、出世運、無病息災など
【特色など】社殿の四方に配された「平安神宮神苑」は名庭として知られる
【所在地】京都市左京区岡崎西天王町

⑯ 住吉大社（大阪）

初詣に200万人が参拝するパワースポット

大阪湾に西面して鎮座する大社の主祭神は、住吉三神と神功皇后。三神はイザナギが禊ぎをしたとき（60ページ）に産まれた天神（底筒男命、中筒男命、表筒男命）で、海の神である。この三神を深く信仰していた神功皇后が建立したのが約1800年前とされ、自らも祭神として祀られた。全国に2300社ある住吉神社の総本社。

【主なご利益】商売繁盛、安産、家内安全、航海守護など

【特色など】祭神を祀る4つの本宮は国宝に指定されている

【所在地】大阪市住吉区住吉

⑮ Heian Jingu (Kyoto)

Built to Commemorate 1,100 Years Since the Establishment of the Capital in Heian (Kyoto)

Following the weakening of Kyoto after the Meiji Restoration, the shrine was built in 1895 with the aim of revitalizing the city. The construction was carried out on a 5/8 scale of the original emperor's palace. The enshrined deity was the 50th emperor, Kanmu, the same as it was when the capital was established in Heian, but in 1940 the 121st emperor, Komei, was also enshrined. The Jidai Matsuri (Festival of the Ages), held every year on October 22, is considered one of Kyoto's three great festivals.

- ◆ **Object of Prayers**: finding a marriage partner, successful promotion, good health without injury, and others.

- ◆ **Features**: The Heian Jingu Gardens, surrounding the shrine on four sides, is particularly famous.

- ◆ **Location**: Okazaki Nishi Tenno-cho, Sakyo-ku, Kyoto.

□ 衰退した fell into decline
□ 復興 revival
□ 大内裏 Inner Palace
□ 8分の5の規模で復元 reconstructed to five-eighths of its original size
□ 合祀された enshrined together
□ 配された situated

⑯ Sumiyoshi Taisha (Osaka)

A Power Spot that Boasts 2,000,000 New Year's Visitors

Facing Osaka bay to the west, the Sumiyoshi shrine is dedicated to the three gods of Sumiyoshi and Empress Jingu. The three gods came into being when Izanagi engaged in an act of purification as described earlier (see page 61). They were the heavenly gods Sokotsutsunoo, Nakatsutsunoo, and Uwatsutsunoo; all were sea gods. Empress Jingu, who was a great believer in these three gods, had the shrine built some 1,800 years ago, with her own name added to the list of enshrined deities. This shrine stands at the head of 2,300 Sumiyoshi Jinjas nationwide.

- ◆ **Object of Prayers**: business prosperity, safe birth, domestic safety, safe voyages, and others.

- ◆ **Features**: Four shrines with enshrined deities are designated national treasures.

- ◆ **Location**: Sumiyoshi, Sumiyoshi-ku, Osaka.

□ 西面する facing west
□ 鎮座する be enshrined
□ 建立する founded

⑰ 西宮神社（兵庫）

90

福の神・えびす様を祀る宮の総本社

　創建は不明だが、主祭神の蛭子大神はイザナギとイザナミの間に最初に産まれた蛭児命とされる（52ページ）。社伝では、西宮に漂着した蛭児命を「夷三郎殿」と称し海をつかさどる神として祀ったという。古代人は、海のかなたからやってくる神は福をもたらすと信じていた。関西では「えべっさん」と、親しみをこめて呼ばれている。

【主なご利益】商売繁盛、金運、開運招福など

【特色など】祭神として、アマテラス、スサノオ、オオクニヌシを祀る

【所在地】兵庫県西宮市社家町

【西宮まつり】例年9月21日（宵宮祭）・22日（例祭）・23日（渡御祭）が催行される。最終日は神輿を乗せた御座船を中心にした船団が巡海して、海の安全を祈願する

　なお、1月10日に催行されるのが、「福男」の座をめざし大勢の男女が競走する「開門神事」だ

西宮まつり　海上渡御祭

Nishinomiya Festival and Cruising Bosts

⑰ Nishinomiya Jinja (Hyogo)

Headquarters of Shrines Dedicated to the God of Wealth (Ebisu-sama)

It is unclear when this shrine was built, but the enshrined deity, Hiruko, was the first child of Izanagi and Izanami (see page 53). According to shrine traditions, when Hiruko was washed ashore at Nishinomiya, he was given the name Ebisu Saburo and enshrined as the deity in charge of the sea. The ancients believe that gods who came from far across the sea brought with them great riches. The people of the Kansai region referred affectionately to the shrine as "Ebessan."

- **Object of Prayers**: business prosperity, financial luck, good prospects and improved fortune, and others.

- **Features**: The enshrined deities are Amaterasu, Susanoo, and Okuninushi.

- **Location**: Shake-cho, Nishinomiya city, Hyogo prefecture.

- **Nishinomiya Festival**: Every year a festival is held on September 21 (the Yoimiya Matsuri), September 22 (the standard matsuri), and September 23 (the portable shrine parade). The final day is highlighted by a fleet of boats carrying portable shrines that makes a tour over the water to pray for safety in the sea.
  On January 10 the "lucky man" race takes place, in which men and women run from the front gate to the main hall to see who will arrive first and be declared the luckiest person for that year.

- □ 創建は不明　the date of its foundation is unknown
- □ 社伝　shrine traditions
- □ 漂着した　washed ashore
- □ 福をもたらす　bring good fortune and prosperity
- □ 渡御　procession of a sacred object
- □ 御座船　a sacred boat used in the festival
- □ 巡海する　sail around the sea
- □ 福男　the first man to reach the shrine on New Year's Day

91

⑱ 氣比神宮（福井）

『古事記』や『日本書紀』にも登場する太古の社

　2000年以上もの歴史をもつとされ、古代には朝廷が**北陸道総鎮守**として特に重視した。当初、伊奢沙別命を主祭神とした。この神は食べ物をつかさどるとされ、『古事記』によると敦賀から朝廷に食べ物が奉じられ、「氣（気）比」という地名は「食の霊」を由来とする。702年、文武天皇の勅命で6柱の祭神が合祀され、今に至る。

　【主なご利益】縁結び、子宝・安産、延命長寿など

　【特色など】1300年前に**噴出**したと伝わる「**長命水**」がパワースポットの一つ

　【所在地】福井県敦賀市曙町

⑲ 白山比咩神社（石川）

全国に2000社以上ある白山信仰の総本社

　石川と岐阜の県境にそびえ立つ白山（2702ｍ）は、古代から崇敬の対象だった。この山を御神体として遥拝する「まつりのにわ」を遷座して社殿を創建したのが716年と伝わる。祭神は、白山比咩大神、伊弉諾尊、伊弉冉尊。白山比咩は、伊弉諾と伊弉冉が黄泉国で**仲たがいしたとき**（52ページ）、間をとりもったとされる菊理媛尊だ。

　【主なご利益】開運招福、縁結び、学業成就、交通安全など

　【特色など】白山の頂上には「奥宮」が鎮座し、一帯は白山国立公園になっている

　【所在地】石川県白山市三宮町

⑱ Kehi Jingu (Fukui)

An Ancient Shrine Mentioned in the *Kojiki* and *Nihon Shoki*

Said to have a history of over 2,000 years, Kehi shrine found particular favor with the ancient imperial court, which made it the tutelary god for the entire Hokuriku region. At the beginning, the enshrined god was Izasawake, who presided over food and, according to the *Kojiki*, had food delivered from Tsuruga to the court. *Kehi* ultimately means "food spirit." In 702 Emperor Monmu ordered that six more gods be added to the enshrinement list, which is the number in effect today.

- **Object of Prayers**: finding a marriage partner, blessed with many children and easy births, a long and healthy life, and others.

- **Features**: One of the shrine's power spots is a 1,300-year-old natural spring whose water ensures a long life.

- **Location**: Akebono-cho, Tsuruga city, Fukui prefecture.

□北陸道 Hokuriku region
□奉じる enshrine
□食の霊 deity of food
□噴出する gush out
□長命水 water of longevity

⑲ Shirayama Hime Jinja (Ishikawa)

The Headquarters of over 2,000 Hakusan Faith Shrines

Lying on the border between Ishikawa and Gifu prefectures, 2,702-meter Mount Hakusan has been revered since the ancient past. It is recorded that a temple was built in 716 so that the mountain could be worshipped from a distance. The principal enshrined gods are Shirayama Hime, Izanagi, and Izanami. When Izanagi and Izanami had their falling out at the world of the dead (see page 53), it was Shirayama Hime (AKA Kukuri Hime) who intervened.

- **Object of Prayers**: good prospects and improved fortune, finding a marriage partner, academic success, traffic safety, and others.

- **Features**: On the top of Mount Hakusan is Okumiya shrine, and the surrounding area comprises Hakusan National Park.

- **Location**: Sannomiya-machi, Hakusan, Ishikawa prefecture.

□県境 border between two prefectures
□まつりのにわ a sacred place where the gods dwell
□遷座する move to a new location
□仲たがいする quarrel
□間をとりもつ intervene

⑳ 出雲大社（島根）

あらゆる縁結びをつかさどる大神を祀る

創建の経緯は『古事記』が伝える（86ページ）。同書では「天之御舎」と記し、8世紀初めには壮大な社殿が建っていたことを物語っている。主祭神は大国主大神（74ページ）で、古来、福をもたらす「だいこく様」として崇敬されてきた。各地に分霊を祀る神社があるが、東京分祀（港区）はコンクリート3階建てだ。

【主なご利益】縁結び、開運など

【特色など】本殿は国宝とされ、60年に一度の「大遷宮」を2019年3月に完遂した

【所在地】島根県出雲市大社町

【参拝方法】出雲大社での拝礼の基本動作は他の神社（134ページ）とは異なり、「二礼四拍手一礼」だ
なお、参拝は①拝殿で拝礼、②瑞垣に沿って摂社・末社を参拝、③神座正面から再度、拝礼、という順序でおこなう
神楽殿には日本最大の注連縄がある

出雲大社　神楽殿
Sacred *shimenawa* rope hanging in front of the Kaguraden

⑳ Izumo Oyashiro (Shimane)
The God who Oversees all Manner of Fateful Meetings

The story of the establishment of Izumo Oyashiro (popularly known as Izumo Taisha) is told in the *Kojiki* (see page 87). The same book describes it as "a heavenly august abode," and relates that magnificent buildings stood on the grounds at the beginning of the 8th century. The chief enshrined god is Okuninushi (see page 75). From the past he has been known as Daikokuten, or Daikoku-sama, and venerated as the god of wealth. His spirit has been divided and re-enshrined throughout the country; the branch shrine in Minato-ku, Tokyo, is a three-story concrete building.

- **Object of Prayers**: finding a marriage partner, developing good fortune, and others.

- **Features**: The main hall is a national treasure. The shrine is renovated every sixty years, the last renovation being completed in March 2019.

- **Location**: Taisha-machi, Izumo city, Shimane prefecture.

- **Prayer Hall**: The action of praying at Izumo Oyashiro is basically different from other shrines (see page 135). It consists of two bows, four claps of the hands, and one bow.
  Further, the order in which the act of worship is conducted is a follows: 1) praying at the prayer hall, 2) praying at the *sessha* and *massha* shrines along the sacred fence, and 3) praying again in front of the "divine seat" (*shinza*) containing the enshrined object.
  The Kaguraden (Sacred Dance Hall) features the largest *shimenawa* sacred rope in the country.

□経緯 history

□同書 the aforementioned book

□大遷宮 the ritual of transferring the deities of the main shrine to a temporary shrine while the main shrine undergoes major renovations

□完遂する fulfill

□瑞垣 sacred fence

□神楽殿 Kagura Hall

㉑嚴島神社（広島）

93

神域の島に建つ世界文化遺産の宮

　日本三景の一つ「安芸の宮島」は、島全体が御神体だ。この島に、市杵島姫命を祭神とする社が創建されたのは593年と伝わる。現在の社殿の原型は、平清盛が1168年頃に寄進造営したもので、現在は6棟が国宝に、14棟が国の重要文化財に指定されている。祭神は、市杵島姫命と妹の田心姫命・湍津姫命の「宗像三女神」（210ページ）である。

【主なご利益】開運、勝運、海上守護、交通安全など

【特色など】世界文化遺産「嚴島神社」（1996年登録）は、神社の背後の弥山を含む
　　一帯（宮島の約14％）

【所在地】広島県廿日市市宮島町

【大鳥居】海上の朱色の大鳥居は、自らの重みで立っている。満潮時は社殿の床下
　　まで海面がせまるが、干潮時には海底が現れて社殿の沖のほうにある大鳥居ま
　　で歩いて行けるようになる
　　なお宮島に生息している鹿は、春日大社（188ページ）のように神使とはされてい
　　ない

嚴島神社　大鳥居
Itsukushima Shrine with *torii* gate "floating" in the ocean

㉑ Itsukushima Jinja (Hiroshima)

A World Heritage Shrine Part of a Sacred Island Complex

Known as one of the three most scenic spots in Japan and also as "the chief shrine of Aki province" (now Western Hiroshima prefecture), the entire island is considered a deity. With Ichikishimahime as its enshrined deity, the shrine is believed to have been built in 593. The present state of the shrine is due to contributions made by Taira no Kiyomori in 1168. Six of its buildings are national treasures, and fourteen are important cultural properties. The enshrined deities are Ichikishimahime, her younger sister Tagorihime, and Tagitsuhime—known as the three Munakata goddesses (see page 211).

- **Object of Prayers**: improvement in one's fortune, good luck in competition, maritime safety, traffic safety, and others.

- **Features**: The Itsukushima shrine complex was designated a World Heritage Site in 1996, including Mount Misen and about 14 percent of the island.

- **Location**: Miyajima-cho, Hatsukaichi city, Hiroshima prefecture.

- **Great *Torii***: The Great Gate, or *Otorii*, sometimes appears to be floating in the sea but it is actually held in place by its own weight. At high tide the water reaches the floorboards of the shrine, but at low tide the seabed appears, allowing visitors to walk out as far as the *torii*.
  Incidentally, the deer on the island are not, like Kasuga Taisha, considered messengers of the gods (see page 189).

□日本三景 Three Most Scenic Spots of Japan

□御神体 the sacred object of worship

□原型 original form

□朱色の vermilion

□自らの重みで立っている standing by its own weight

□満潮 high tide

□干潮 low tide

94

㉒ 金刀比羅宮（香川）

四国随一のパワースポット「こんぴらさん」

香川県の象頭山中腹に鎮座する神社で、創建年代は諸説ある。当初からの主祭神の金毘羅神は仏教の守護神クンピーラとされ、**鰐の神格化だったことで海神や龍神に比定された**。のちに主祭神を大物主神としたが、これは金毘羅神の真実の姿を現したもの。江戸時代中期には「金毘羅参り」が大流行し、全国にその名が広まった。

【**主なご利益**】開運、商売繁盛、航海守護、農業守護など

【**特色など**】総本宮まで785段、奥宮まで1368段の石段を登る

【**所在地**】香川県仲多度郡琴平町字川西

㉓ 大山祇神社（愛媛）

山の神、海の神、酒の神として崇敬される古社

瀬戸内海の大三島の鷲ヶ頭山の**西麓**に鎮座する神社で、山を御神体とする。創建は594年と伝わり、主祭神は大山積大神。この神は、その名のように山をつかさどるだけでなく海や酒の神でもあり、天孫ニニギの妻コノハナサクヤヒメの父神だ（98ページ）。平氏や源氏の**武将**が武具を奉納したことで、**武の神**としても崇敬された。

【**主なご利益**】縁結び、開運、勝運、海上守護など

【**特色など**】全国に1万社余りある「山祇神社」「三島神社」の総本社

【**所在地**】愛媛県今治市三島町宮浦

㉒ **Kotohiragu (Kagawa)**
Shikoku's Preeminent Power Spot—Konpira-san

Located halfway up Mount Zozu in Kagawa prefecture, there are a number of theories about the date of the shrine's erection. From the beginning the principal enshrined god was Konpira, who was the Buddhist guardian god Kumbhīra. Kumbhīra was a deification of the crocodile and identified with the god of the sea and the dragon god. Later Omononushi became the chief enshrined god, which was said to be Konpira's true form. In the middle of the Edo period visiting the shrine (*konpira-mairi*) enjoyed great popularity, and the name of the shrine spread throughout the country.

- **Object of Prayers**: improved fortunes, business prosperity, maritime safety, protection of crops, and others.

- **Features**: It is a climb of 785 stone steps to the main shrine and 1,368 to the inner shrine.

- **Location**: Kotohira-cho, Nakatado-gun, Kagawa prefecture.

□ クンピーラ Kumbhīra (a Hindu water deity often depicted as a crocodile)
□ 鰐 crocodile
□ 神格化 deification
□ 海神 god of the sea
□ 龍神 dragon god
□ 〜に比定された be identified with
□ 石段 stone steps

㉓ **Oyamazumi Jinja (Ehime)**
Long Venerated as a Mountain God, Sea God, and Sake God

Situated on the western foot of the mountain Washigatozan on the island of Omishima in the Seto Inland Sea, the shrine takes the mountain itself as its sacred object. Said to have been built in 594, its enshrined god is Oyamazumi. Oyamazumi is the god of mountains as well as the sea and sake. He is the father of Konohanasakuyahime, wife of Ninigi (see page 99). Due to the offerings of military equipment made by the Taira and Minamoto families, Oyamazumi is also honored as the god of war.

- **Object of Prayers**: finding a marriage partner, improving good fortune, greater competitive luck, maritime safety, and others.

- **Features**: Headquarters of over 10,000 Yamazumi and Mishima shrines.

- **Location**: Miyaura, Mishima-cho, Imabari city, Ehime prefecture.

□ 西麓 western foothills
□ 武将 warlord
□ 奉納する dedicate
□ 武の神 god of war

95

㉔香椎宮（福岡）

神功皇后が亡き天皇のために建てた祠が起源

福岡市北部の立花山南西麓に鎮座する古社。社伝によると、創建は724年。それより古くには霊廟だったとされ、『古事記』は「訶志比宮」と記す。主祭神は、14代仲哀天皇と神功皇后。天皇は熊襲討伐の途中で急死したため、皇后自ら香椎に祠を建てて祀ったのを起源とする。その経緯は神話として、『古事記』の「仲哀記」に詳しい。

【主なご利益】勝運、開運招福、安産・子育て守護など

【特色など】配祀神として、応神天皇（15代）と住吉大神が祀られている

【所在地】福岡市東区香椎

㉕太宰府天満宮（福岡）

菅原道真の霊廟としても崇敬を集める「天神さま」

菅原道真公が主祭神の天満宮、北野神社、菅原神社、天神社は全国に約1万2000社あるという。これらは、北野天満宮（190ページ）と太宰府天満宮のいずれかへの勧請によるものだ。太宰府天満宮は、左遷されて当地に赴き、無念の思いで死を迎えた道真の埋葬地の上に建立（919年）されたという点で意義深い。

【主なご利益】受験合格、学業成就、厄除け、病気平癒など

【特色など】参拝者は年間1000万人。受験生に人気のパワースポットだ

【所在地】福岡県太宰府市大宰府

㉔ **Kashiigu (Fukuoka)**

Rising from a Sanctum Built by Empress Jingu for Her Departed Husband

Kashiigu has been situated from old on the southwest foot of Mount Tachibana in the northern part of Fukuoka city. According to shrine records, it was built in 724. Before that, it was a mausoleum, and the *Kojiki* refers to it as Kashii no Miya (Chinquapin Shrine). It is dedicated to the spirits of the 14th emperor, Chuai, and the empress Jingu. The emperor suddenly died while fighting a tribe called the Kumaso, and the empress built a mausoleum dedicated to him using the aromatic chinquapin trees growing nearby. This is said to be the origin of the name of the shrine. This story is told in the *Kojiki* in the section called "Record of Chuai."

◆ **Object of Prayers**: greater competitive luck, good prospects and improved fortune, easy childbirth, safe childrearing, and others.

◆ **Features**: Kashiigu also enshrines the spirits of the 15th emperor, Ojin, and the Great God of Sumiyoshi.

◆ **Location**: Kashii, Higashi-ku, Fukuoka city.

□霊廟 mausoleum

□熊襲 the people of the Kumaso tribe, who are said to have resisted the Yamato kingdom in what is now southern Kyushu in the mythology of the Chronicles of Japan

□祠 small shrine

□配祀神 a deity enshrined alongside the main deity, often a deity with a close relationship to the main deity

㉕ **Dazaifu Tenmangu (Fukuoka)**

The Mausoleum of Sugawara no Michizane: Known and Honored as Tenjin-sama

The number of shrines at which Sugawara no Michizane has been deified—including such as Tenmangu, Kitano Jinja, Sugawara Jinja, and Tenjinsha—exceeds 12,000. All of these are propagations of the Kitano Tenmangu (see page 191) or Dazaifu Tenmangu. When Michizane died after being exiled to faraway Dazaifu due to a political disagreement, a shrine was built over his grave in 919, marking the resting place of the man who would become the god of learning.

◆ **Object of Prayers**: success in entrance exams, academic achievement, avoidance of evil, recovery from illness, and others.

◆ **Features**: There are 10,000,000 visitors a year. It is a well-known power spot among test examinees.

◆ **Location**: Dazaifu, Dazaifu city, Fukuoka prefecture.

□AとBのいずれかへの勧請による due to requests to either A or B

□当地に赴く be sent to this region

□無念の思いで死を迎える die with unfulfilled desires

□埋葬地 burial place

□意義深い profound

96

㉖宗像大社（福岡）

最高神を意味する「貴」の称号をもつ宗像大神を祀る

　創建は不明だが、主祭神の宗像大神（宗像三女神）が天上界の最高神アマテラスの御子神（市杵島姫神、湍津姫神、田心姫神）ということで大社の称号を「道主貴」とする。これは、伊勢神宮（おおひるめのむち）、出雲大社（おおなむち）と並ぶ最高位にランクされていたということ。神宝として古代祭祀の国宝を多数有しているのもその証左である。

【主なご利益】海上安全、商売繁盛、勝運、芸事上達、子孫繁栄など

【特色など】2017年、大社は「神宿る島」宗像・沖ノ島と関連遺産群の一つとして、世界文化遺産に登録された

【所在地】福岡県宗像市

【宗像大社】市杵島姫神を祀る「辺津宮」、そこから11km先に湍津姫神を祀る「中津宮」、さらに49km先に田心姫神を祀る「沖津宮」がある。朝鮮半島の釜山までは145kmの近距離で、古代から海上路による大陸との交流が盛んだった

宗像大社 沖津宮
Okitsugu, Munakata Taisha

㉖ Munakata Taisha (Fukuoka)
Enshrining the Supreme Goddesses of Munakata

The date the shrine was built is uncertain, but the enshrined deities are the daughters of Amaterasu (Ichikishimahime, Tagitsuhime, and Tagorihime). The shrine is also known as Michinushi-no-muchi. The appellation *muchi* ranks the shrine along with Ise Jingu (Ohirume-no-muchi) and Izumo Oyashiro (Onamuchi) as being of the highest divine level. This is evidenced by the great number of its enshrined national treasures.

◆ **Object of Prayers**: maritime safety, business prosperity, luck in competition, improvement in artistic endeavors, affluent descendants, and others.

◆ **Features**: In 2017 the shrine was designated a World Heritage Site as part of the Sacred Island of Okinoshima and Associated Sites in the Munakata Region.

◆ **Location**: Munakata city, Fukuoka prefecture.

◆ **Munakata Taisha**: Ichikishimahime is enshrined in Hetsugu; 11 kilometers further on, Tagitsuhime is enshrined in Nakatsugu; and 49 kilometers beyond that, Tagorihime is enshrined in Okitsugu. Just a short 145 kilometers from this point is Busan on the Korean peninsula, marking off a trade route that was active since olden times.

□御子神 deity regarded as the child of the main deity enshrined at the same shrine

□称号 honorific title

□古代祭祀 ancient religious ceremonies

□証左 evidence

□「神宿る島」宗像・沖ノ島と関連遺産群 Sacred Island of Okinoshima and Associated Sites in the Munakata Region

□釜山 Busan

97

㉗宇佐神宮（大分）

4万余りの「八幡さま」の総本宮で、御神輿の発祥地

国東半島の付け根に立つ御許山の山麓に鎮座する神宮には、三つの御殿がある。一之御殿は725年の創建で祭神は八幡大神（応神天皇）、二之御殿は733年の創建で祭神は比売大神（宗像三女神）、三之御殿は823年の創建で祭神は神功皇后（114ページ）。奈良時代以降、天皇の崇敬を受け、皇室の宗廟の一つとされた。

【主なご利益】仕事運、縁結び、安産、子育てなど

【特色など】参拝は、出雲大社と同様に「二礼四拍手一礼」の作法でおこなう

【所在地】大分県宇佐市南宇佐

㉘鵜戸神宮（宮崎）

初代神武天皇の父神を主祭神とする洞窟内の古社

日向灘に面した洞窟の中に鎮座する神宮で、社伝によると創建は10代崇神天皇の世とされる。主祭神は彦波瀲武鸕鷀草葺不合尊で、アマテラスの5代目の子孫にあたる（106ページ）。「ウド」とは内部が空洞になった場所を意味し、祭神名にみられる「鸕鷀」は鳥の鵜である。1875年、神宮号が宣下されて現社名になった。

【主なご利益】縁結び、子授け、安産など

【特色など】境内の「亀石」は霊石とされ、運玉を亀の背のくぼみに投げ入れられたら願いが成就するという

【所在地】宮崎県日南市宮浦

㉗ Usa Jingu (Oita)

Headquarters of over 40,000 "Hachiman-sama" Shrines and Birthplace of the *Mikoshi* (Portable Shrine)

Situated at the foot of Mount Omoto on the neck of Kunisaki peninsula, Usa Jingu consists of three shrine buildings. The first was erected in 725 and is dedicated to the god Hachiman (i.e., Emperor Ojin). The second was built in 733 and enshrines the deity Hime (i.e., the three goddess of Munakata). The third was built in 823 and is dedicated to the empress Jingu (see page 115). From the Nara period onward, Usa Jingu received the patronage of the emperor and was made a mausoleum of the imperial household.

- ❖ **Object of Prayers**: good fortune in work, finding a marriage partner, easy birth, safe childrearing, and others.

- ❖ **Features**: The act of prayer is the same as at Izumo Oyashiro: two bows, four claps, and one bow.

- ❖ **Location**: Minami Usa, Usa city, Oita prefecture.

□〜の付け根 at the tip of
□山麓 mountain foothills
□御殿 main shrine building

㉘ Udo Jingu (Miyazaki)

An Ancient Cavern Shrine Dedicated to the Father of the First Emperor

Situated in a cavern facing the Hyuganada Sea, Udo Jingu was built in the time of the 10th emperor Sujin, according to shrine records. The principal enshrined god is Hikonagisatakeugayafukiaezu, a fifth-generation descendant of Amaterasu (see page 107). The word *udo* in the name of the shrine refers to a hollowed-out area, and the characters 鸕鷀 in the name of the enshrined deity mean "cormorant." In 1875 the name the shrine was changed by imperial decree to the name it has today.

- ❖ **Object of Prayers**: finding a marriage partner, childrearing, safe childbirth, and others.

- ❖ **Features**: Within the precincts of the shrine there is a sacred rock in the shape of a turtle, and if a visitor manages to toss a "fortune jewel" onto the hollow in the back of the turtle, his or her wish will come true.

- ❖ **Location**: Miyaura, Nichinan city, Miyazaki prefecture.

□洞窟 sea cave
□内部が空洞になった場所 natural cave
□鵜 cormorant
□神宮号が宣下される granted the title of Jingu
□亀石 turtle rock
□霊石 sacred rock
□運玉 fortune stone

Read Real NIHONGO

日本の神々
The Gods of Japan

2024年5月5日　第1刷発行

著　者　安部　直文

訳　者　マイケル・ブレーズ

発行者　賀川　洋

発行所　IBCパブリッシング株式会社
　　　　〒162-0804 東京都新宿区中里町29番3号　菱秀神楽坂ビル
　　　　Tel. 03-3513-4511　Fax. 03-3513-4512
　　　　www.ibcpub.co.jp

印刷所　株式会社シナノパブリッシングプレス

ISBN978-4-7946-0810-9